COMPLETE

FIRST
for Schools

Workbook
without answers

with Audio Download

Second edition

B2

WITH AUDIO
DOWNLOAD

Natasha de Souza

Cambridge University Press
www.cambridge.org/elt

Cambridge Assessment English
www.cambridgeenglish.org

Information on this title: www.cambridge.org/9781108647427

First published 2019

20 19 18 17 16 15 14 13 12 11 10 9 8 7 6

Printed in Poland by Opolgraf

A catalogue record for this publication is available from the British Library

ISBN 978-1-108-72469-2 Workbook with Audio download

Contents

1 A family affair

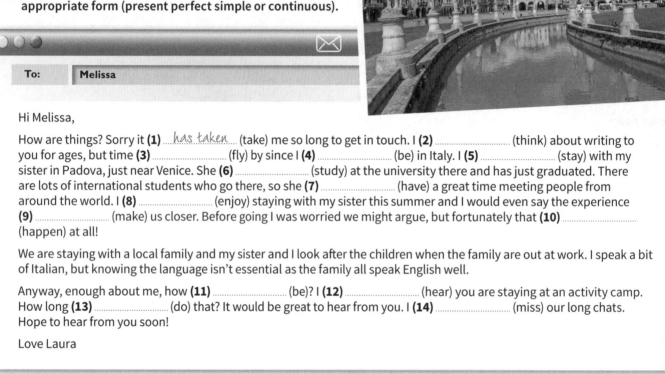

Grammar

Present perfect simple and continuous

1 Read this email and put the verbs in brackets into the most appropriate form (present perfect simple or continuous).

To: Melissa

Hi Melissa,

How are things? Sorry it **(1)** ...has taken... (take) me so long to get in touch. I **(2)** .... (think) about writing to you for ages, but time **(3)** .... (fly) by since I **(4)** .... (be) in Italy. I **(5)** .... (stay) with my sister in Padova, just near Venice. She **(6)** .... (study) at the university there and has just graduated. There are lots of international students who go there, so she **(7)** .... (have) a great time meeting people from around the world. I **(8)** .... (enjoy) staying with my sister this summer and I would even say the experience **(9)** .... (make) us closer. Before going I was worried we might argue, but fortunately that **(10)** .... (happen) at all!

We are staying with a local family and my sister and I look after the children when the family are out at work. I speak a bit of Italian, but knowing the language isn't essential as the family all speak English well.

Anyway, enough about me, how **(11)** .... (be)? I **(12)** .... (hear) you are staying at an activity camp. How long **(13)** .... (do) that? It would be great to hear from you. I **(14)** .... (miss) our long chats. Hope to hear from you soon!

Love Laura

Asking questions (present perfect simple and continuous)

2 A few days later, Laura replies to Melissa and asks her the following questions in her email. Use the prompts to write her questions using the most appropriate form (present perfect simple or continuous) in the speech balloons.

1 how long / stay / with the family?

> How long have you been staying with the family?

2 Italian / improve a lot?

> ....

3 make / lots of new friends?

> ....

4 you visit / other parts of Italy yet?

> ....

5 what / weather / like?

> ....

6 eat / lots of delicious ice cream?

> ....

Vocabulary

Collocations with *make* and *do*

1 Complete each of the sentences below with the correct form of *make* or *do*.

1 Before going to Italy, Melissa ....*did*.... a course in Italian.

2 In order to get pocket money the kids have to .... jobs.

3 My parents get really mad if I .... a mess before guests arrive.

4 My brother is .... dinner tonight, I hope it tastes OK!

5 I have .... a promise to my sister that I will always keep.

6 I can't see you tonight. I'm .... something with my cousin. We are going to the cinema.

7 When we go to my aunt's house we have to .... our homework before dinner.

8 I have .... the decision to visit my grandmother every weekend.

9 Because they are twins, I sometimes .... the mistake of speaking to the wrong sister.

10 My mum always .... her food shopping online.

Adjectives

2 For each of the sentences below, make an adjective from one of the words in the box. Some gaps need a negative adjective.

relief think energy believe ~~pride~~
entertain ambition

1 He was too ....*proud*.... to ask his parents for help.

2 She thought her brother's show was very .... She hadn't enjoyed herself so much for a long time.

3 He was .... when his brother arrived home safely.

4 He was very .... and was determined to do better than his siblings.

5 He is so unlike his twin brother. It's .... that they are even related.

6 She is a very .... child and always considers how other people feel.

7 Even though their grandmother is in her seventies, she is still fairly .... and often goes to the gym.

Phrasal verbs

3 Complete each gap with a phrasal verb which means the same as the word(s) in brackets. Use the verbs in the box in their correct form.

wear out ~~take on~~ clear up cheer up
tear up hang around with

Last week we welcomed a new addition to our family and
(1) ....*took on*............ (accept responsibility) a puppy called Toby. Having him around has had its advantages and disadvantages, but for the most part I've really enjoyed it. On the plus side, he is great company and always manages to
(2) .... (make happy) when I come in from school. Also, having him means I always have someone to
(3) .... (spend time with). He has a lot of energy, so I have to **(4)** .... (make tired) by taking him for regular walks. The only downside to having Toby, is that it is also a lot of hard work! Because he is still very young he sometimes tries to **(5)** .... (destroy) the furniture and he makes a big mess, which I then have to **(6)** .... (tidy).

Writing Part 2

An article

Read part of an article written by a student for a magazine and correct the spelling and punctuation. There are 12 mistakes. The first one has been corrected for you.

Staying with your grandparents is great when you

are ~~growed~~ *growing* up. When my brother and I visit are

grandparents they are always really pleased to see

us. My parents say we get spoilt when we stay there,

but they dont seem to mind to much. During the

school holidays our grandparents always give us nice

things to eat, and sometimes its food we havent tryed

before. They also tell us a lot of intresting stories

about there past and things which happened before

we were born. The best stories are always about

our parents' and how they behaved when they were

young. Our grandparents also do lots of enjoyable

things with us, such as taking us to the beach or the

park. Last time we visited, we made cake's and went

swimming. Even though they are in they're seventies,

they are still very active!

1

Listening Part 3

Read A–H and listen carefully to each speaker. The words you hear will be different from those below.

Exam Info

🎧 02 You will hear five short extracts in which teenagers describe their favourite family holiday. For questions 1–5, choose from the list (A–H) what each speaker says about the holiday. Use the letters only once. There are three extra letters which you do not need to use.

A I regret arguing on holiday.

B I'm going to try to have the same experience but with different people.

C I felt more independent on this trip.

D I enjoyed the holiday because we stayed in a posh hotel.

E I wish I had done more on this holiday.

F My enjoyment of this holiday largely relied on us having good weather.

G I am fortunate that this trip was captured on film.

H I didn't enjoy the holiday when it rained.

Speaker 1 [ ] **1**

Speaker 2 [ ] **2**

Speaker 3 [ ] **3**

Speaker 4 [ ] **4**

Speaker 5 [ ] **5**

Reading and Use of English Part 7

Read the questions, then quickly read the texts. When you find the part of a text which matches the question, underline it.

Exam Info

You are going to read a newspaper article about being a twin. For questions 1–10, choose from the people (A–E). The people may be chosen more than once.

Which person

appreciates the importance of twins needing to find their own way in life? **1** [ ]

has mixed feelings about being looked after by their sibling? **2** [ ]

feels angry when people assume that all twins look the same? **3** [ ]

likes having conversations about being a twin? **4** [ ]

didn't like the way they were viewed as a twin child? **5** [ ]

struggles when parted from their sibling? **6** [ ]

realises that it is not only twins who sometimes argue? **7** [ ]

no longer has a problem with being a twin? **8** [ ]

shares their parents, view of being a twin? **9** [ ]

has always felt fortunate to be a twin? **10** [ ]

*sibling: a sister or brother

The pros and cons of being a twin

A Sam Pearson, 13

People often ask: 'What's it like being a twin?' To which I often respond, 'I don't know. I have never been anything else!' I never mean to be rude; I am just being honest because since birth I have never known anything different. I guess there are some advantages though, for example, there is always someone to partner you in class or hang around with at home. Also, when I meet new people they always find it really interesting to talk about what it must be like being a twin.

B Julia Taylor, 30

I have always loved being a twin and I see being one as something unique. There aren't many people who have had this benefit and therefore I try to always focus on the positives. This is something our mum and dad taught us when we were very young and I have always remembered this. When we were growing up, one of the best things about being a twin was our birthday parties! We had brilliant birthdays as kids. I am sure they were fairly stressful for our parents, but we thought they were fabulous!

C Claire Kite, 16

People often presume when you are a twin that you must also be identical. This is not the case however, and my twin brother is much taller than me; so sometimes people don't believe we are twins and I find this really annoying! Being a twin has both its good and bad points. We fight a lot, especially over gadgets, and when we were younger over toys or for the attention of our parents, but I guess this is just like any other family. On the positive side, we often have a lot of fun together and I never feel lonely. My brother is also very protective of me, especially at school, which is both a good and bad thing!

D Mary Blackwell, 40

Growing up I had very mixed emotions about being a twin. I really hated it when people grouped us, referring to us as 'the twins'! We very much had our own identities and some people just failed to recognise that. I used to constantly dye my hair different colours, just so I could look different to my sister. Being seen as a unit rather than as an individual didn't seem to bother my sister that much, but for some reason it really affected me, especially as a teenager. Fortunately, we now have very different lives, so it isn't really an issue anymore.

E Helen Thompson, 19

I absolutely loved being a twin when I was growing up. I used to have a great time going out with my sister. We are identical, so we always used to wear the same clothes and have the same haircuts. We got so much attention when we went out and we were sometimes asked to pose for photographs. We felt like celebrities! We were also very close when we were younger, and sure we would argue sometimes, but most of the time we were best friends. This has all changed now though, as we have each gone to a different university. I know it is a good idea that we each have our own independence, but I do find it hard sometimes and a bit lonely.

2 Leisure and pleasure

Grammar

Making comparisons

1 **Circle the correct comparative or superlative form.**

1 Water skiing is probably the *more* / (*most*) daring activity I have ever done.
2 Playing the drums is much more enjoyable *then* / *than* playing any other instrument.
3 Tom enjoys going bowling, but he doesn't play as *well* / *good* as his sister.
4 Winter is far *more better* / *better* than summer, because I can go sledging.
5 I am the *least* / *less* musical person in my family.
6 Learning how to ski, was *more easy* / *easier* than I had imagined.
7 It was the *worse* / *worst* football match I had ever seen.
8 I am not as sporty *than* / *as* my sister.

2 **Some of these sentences contain mistakes. Correct the mistakes and put a tick ✓ next to the sentences which are correct.**

1 Going to the cinema is more interesting than staying at home to watch a film. ✓
2 My ~~less~~ *least* favourite sport is golf.
3 This was the bigest event the town had ever hosted.
4 The concert ticket was cheaper than I thought it would be.
5 Drawing is the more relaxing way to spend your free time.
6 The opposing team were more friendlier than I had expected.
7 Cricket is most interesting to play than to watch on television.
8 The easiest way to have a healthy lifestyle is to stay active in your free time.

Adjectives with -ed and -ing

3 **Complete the words to form adjectives with -ed or -ing.**

1 The basketball game was really interest............ to watch.
2 I have always been fascinat............ by martial arts.
3 He was absolutely thrill............ by his achievement in the competition.
4 It was really embarrass............ when she turned up for the party a day late.
5 I find painting really relax............ when I am listening to music.
6 She had never been interest............ in climbing.

4 **Complete the table with the verb and noun forms.**

Adjective	Verb	Noun
annoyed / annoying	to annoy	annoyance
confused / confusing		
fascinated / fascinating		
frustrated / frustrating		
embarrassed / embarrassing		
irritating / irritated		
satisfied / satisfying		
surprised / surprising		
worried / worrying		

Writing Part 2

Organising ideas into paragraphs
Compound and complex sentences

1 Read the sentences about an activity called 'Zorb' football. Make complex sentences by joining the sentences in each line with *and*, *but* or *because*.

1 I thought I would enjoy it. Really didn't know what to expect.

2 I would definitely do it again. I recommend it to anyone who wants to have a bit of fun!

3 Two weeks ago I tried a new activity called Zorb football. It was amazing.

4 However, after just a short time, I soon began to really enjoy myself. It isn't suitable for anyone wanting a serious game of football. We had a great laugh bumping into each other.

5 Before going I was excited. I was also intrigued. I have always been interested in football.

6 I had seen it advertised months ago. Only tried it recently for a friend's birthday.

7 Zorb football is basically playing football whilst wearing a large inflatable ball which fits over your head and body. Legs are left free, so players can easily move around the pitch.

8 When we first began playing I wasn't sure what I thought. It was so different to normal football.

2 Now look at the exam task and a student's plan below. Match the combined sentences (1–8) from a student's answer to the correct paragraphs (A–C).

This month's writing competition:

NEW EXPERIENCES!

Tell us about an activity you have recently tried out for the first time.

> What was it? Why did you decide to try it?

> What does the activity involve?

> How did you feel before trying it?

> Did you enjoy it? Why / why not?

> Would you recommend it? Why / why not?

We will publish the most interesting articles in next month's issue.

Student's plan

A Paragraph 1: Introduction – the name of the new activity and why you tried it
Sentences ....3........ ....

B Paragraph 2: Description of activity, feeling before trying it
Sentences ....

C Paragraph 3: Was it enjoyable? / Would I recommend it?
Sentences ....

Vocabulary

Phrasal verbs with *up*

1 Which of these things can you *set up*, *give up*, *make up* or *take up*? Write the words under the correct phrasal verb.

~~a sport~~   chocolate   a story   a meeting
a business   hope   camp   an excuse

set up	give up	make up	take up
			a sport

2

Phrasal verbs with *off*

2 Match the phrasal verbs with their definitions.

1	take off	**A**	to suddenly stop speaking or doing something
2	call off	**B**	to give all the money that you owe
3	wear off	**C**	to suddenly start to be successful or popular
4	see off	**D**	when a feeling or the effect of something gradually disappears
5	break off	**E**	to decide that a planned activity will not take place
6	pay off	**F**	to go to the place where someone is leaving to say goodbye

3 Complete each sentence with the correct form of one of the phrasal verbs in Exercise 2.

1 She had to ....*break off*.... what she was doing due to an unexpected emergency.

2 My friends came to the station in order to .... my cousin when she went home.

3 It has taken me a long time to .... the loan for my bike.

4 Zorb football has really .... in my area and now a few clubs have been set up.

5 I usually feel exhausted after a race and it takes at least a day or so for the tiredness to ....

6 Organisers had to .... the concert at the last minute, due to bad weather.

Listening Part 4

 You will hear an interview with Tyler Williams, a professional dancer. For questions 1–7, choose the best answer (A, B or C).

1 Why was Tyler interested in dancing as a child?
   A Dancing had always been in his family.
   B He enjoyed watching dancers on the street.
   C He was influenced by watching movies.

2 Tyler started giving street performances
   A to practise the moves he had learnt as a child.
   B to earn some extra money.
   C because his friend suggested it.

3 How did Tyler react at first when his friend posted one of his dance performances online?
   A He was very angry with him for doing this.
   B He was happy that his sister liked his performance.
   C It confirmed how he felt about his ability.

4 How did Tyler's parents feel about his choice of career? They felt
   A excited for him, as they realised he had the potential to do well.
   B worried about Tyler being able to always find work.
   C lucky, because their son was so talented.

5 What was the main reason Tyler enjoyed attending the academy?
   A He learnt new dance styles, such as ballet and tap.
   B He developed his own dance style even more.
   C He was encouraged to invent his own dances.

6 Tyler had practice performing outside of the school because
   A the academy wanted to encourage Tyler even more.
   B the academy had a good relationship with other dance schools.
   C the academy had a good relationship with venues in the nearby area.

7 After graduating, Tyler feels lucky because he
   A gets to tour around the country.
   B has always had a job.
   C because he is starring in a West End show.

Phrasal verbs with *off*

Reading and Use of English Part 2

For questions 1–8, read the text below and think of the word which best fits each gap. Use only one word in each gap. There is an example at the beginning (0).

50 THINGS TO DO BEFORE YOU'RE 11³/⁴

In April 2012, a UK-based organisation, responsible for conservation projects (the National Trust), set **(0)** ......up...... a nationwide scheme **(1)** .... encourage children to spend more time outdoors. The idea called '50 Things to do Before You're 11¾' came **(2)** .... response to a report which highlighted a severe decline **(3)** .... the amount of time children are spending outdoors. Research revealed that fewer **(4)** .... one in ten children regularly played outside **(5)** .... comparison to just half a generation ago. Furthermore, **(6)** .... report found that a third of children have never climbed a tree and one in ten cannot ride a bike. This new plan encourages youngsters to spend time outdoors **(7)** .... providing an interesting checklist of things to do outside. Activities include things like setting **(8)** .... a snail race, flying a kite or making a mud pie.

Reading and Use of English Part 4

For questions 1–6, complete the second sentence so that it has a similar meaning to the first sentence, using the word given. Do not change the word given. You must use between two and five words, including the word given. Here is an example (0).

Example:

0 He doesn't enjoy skating as much as skiing.
MORE
He likes .....*skiing more than*..... skating.

1 Team sports are much more enjoyable than individual sports.
NEARLY
Individual sports are
.... team sports.

2 She is better at playing the flute than the violin.
AS
She doesn't play the violin
.... the flute.

3 He ran to the ball faster than his opponent.
REACH
His opponent was ....
the ball than he was.

4 He is better at squash than he is at tennis.
NOT
His tennis .... his squash.

5 Running and rowing are equally challenging activities.
AS
Running is .... rowing.

6 It took him longer to climb the mountain than his brother.
MORE
His brother climbed the mountain
.... than he did.

3 Happy holidays?

Grammar

Past simple, past continuous, past perfect simple and past perfect continuous

1 Read these sentences about a flight from London to New York and put the verbs in brackets into the past simple or the past continuous.

Five years ago, I had the most memorable flight to New York. While we **(1)** ....*were waiting*............ (wait) for the plane to take off, the lady passenger next to me **(2)** .... (ask) if she could borrow a pen. As we **(3)** .... (talk), I realised from her accent that she came from my hometown. We **(4)** .... (chat) constantly throughout the entire eight-hour journey and even **(5)** .... (discover) we had attended the same school, although we **(6)** .... (be / not) in the same year group. This lady was a couple of years older than me, so while I **(7)** .... (study) for my GSCE's, she **(8)** .... (prepare) for her A-level exams. Although we were in different year groups at school, we did have some friends in common. In fact, she **(9)** .... (visit) one of them on this trip! When we **(10)** .... (arrive) in New York, we exchanged numbers and **(11)** .... (promise) to keep in touch. Unfortunately, shortly after, I **(12)** .... (lose) her contact details and she hasn't contacted me.

2 For each gap, put the verb in brackets into the past perfect or the past perfect continuous.

1 Passengers ....*had been waiting*.......... (wait) for over an hour when the pilot announced that there would be further delays.

2 By the age of one, Henry .... (visit) six different countries.

3 For her sixtieth birthday, Margaret decided to go on a cruise, as she .... (not be) on one before.

4 I felt exhausted when I got home because I .... (travel) for two days.

5 When I got to the hotel I realised that I .... (forgot) to pack my toothbrush!

6 Before travelling to India I made sure I .... (have) the necessary vaccinations.

7 She .... (look) at holidays to Australia before she realised they were out of her budget.

3 For each gap, put the verb in brackets into the past simple, past continuous, past perfect simple or past perfect continuous. You will need to make some of the verbs negative.

Our last family holiday was amazing! We **(1)** ....*went*................ (go) on our first activity holiday.
It **(2)** .... (be) a package holiday to Greece and all the activities **(3)** .... (be) included in the price. I **(4)** .... (do) many of the activities on offer, so I was excited to try some of them. **(5)** I .... (go sailing) once before, but **(6)** .... (try) any of the other water sports. By the second day of the holiday **(7)** I .... (build up) enough courage to try water skiing. My legs **(8)** .... (feel) like jelly while the speed boat **(9)** .... (pull) me along, but unbelievably I somehow **(10)** .... (manage) to stay up. The whole experience felt brilliant.
Before going on this trip, the activity I **(11)** .... (look forward to) the most, was tennis. However, by far the best thing about this holiday was trying something new.

at, in and on in time phrases

4 Complete each gap in the email with *at*, *in* or *on*.

Holiday Review ★ ★ ★ ★ ★

This was a truly wonderful holiday – the location and hotel were both perfect for what we wanted. **(1)** ...*At*... this time of year the weather isn't too hot and the town isn't overcrowded. **(2)** .... the summer months it may be a different story. The hotel is located right in the town centre, so it's easy to walk to nearby restaurants and cafés **(3)** .... the evening. **(4)** .... Sundays there is also the street market, full of locals and bargains! The town itself is located on the coast so we had a spectacular view of the sea from our room. **(5)** .... night we would sit on our balcony and admire the scenery.

The hotel also offered a full timetable of entertainment throughout the week, so there was always something to do. **(6)** .... the mornings there would always be some kind of exercise class on offer, and **(7)** .... the afternoons the activity was usually a game or competition of some sort. After dinner, **(8)** .... the evenings, there was always some type of entertainment, either a comedy show or band. **(9)** .... the weekends however, we tended to do our own thing.

I would definitely go again, but perhaps next time **(10)** .... June, when it is perhaps a bit warmer.

Vocabulary

Adjectives

1 Make adjectives from the nouns in brackets.

1 I like to visit ...*historical*... places when I go abroad. (history)

2 The most .... place I have ever visited is Hamilton Island. (magic)

3 Some .... accents can be difficult to understand, even if you do speak the language. (region)

4 The view from my balcony was very .... (picture)

5 When we met at the port in Lisbon it was purely .... (accident)

6 The service on the cruise was quite .... (remark)

7 I don't like to be too .... (ambition) when I travel, I simply want to relax.

8 When I told my parents I wanted to travel for my gap year they were really .... (support)

9 In Japan it is .... (custom) to bow when you meet someone.

10 On holiday you only need to know .... (function) language to get around.

11 The staff working on the resort were very .... (profession)

12 I find .... (east) cooking really tasty.

Travel words

2 Complete the gaps with words from the box.

budget   cultures   hostels   expedition   continent   ~~backpacking~~   tourist   economical   rail   abroad

---

Before going to university I decided to take a gap year and go **(1)** ...*backpacking*... around Europe. I wanted to experience different **(2)** .... before continuing my studies. Like most people my age, I didn't have a big **(3)** .... for this **(4)** .... , so my trip needed to be **(5)** .... So I made the decision early on that I would travel mostly by **(6)** .... and stay in **(7)** .... Having finished my trip, I am so glad I did this. Now I have travelled **(8)** .... , I definitely feel more confident.

While travelling I tried not to be too much of a **(9)** .... by trying to interact with the local people as much as possible. I wanted to get a real insight into the place I was visiting. I enjoyed it so much and I am planning to go again, perhaps to a different **(10)** .... this time, like Asia!

3

Word formation

3 Write the adjectives of the words in the left-hand column in the correct columns in the table below.
One example has been done for you.

Adjective	-ive	-ical	-eous	-ing	-ful	-able	-al
1 act	*Active*						
2 comfort							
3 ourage							
4 emotion							
5 economy							
6 annoy							
7 enjoy							
8 pain							
9 predict							
10 encourage							

4 Replace the underlined words in the following sentences with a word from the table.

1 I don't feel <u>relaxed</u> in a country where I don't know the language.
comfortable

2 Going on holiday in the winter can be very <u>cheap</u>.

3 I got sunburnt on my last holiday and my skin was <u>really hurting me</u>.

4 Being delayed at an airport is very <u>irritating</u>.

5 I think you have to be quite <u>brave</u> to go travelling alone.

6 Saying goodbye at the airport can sometimes be very <u>upsetting</u>.

7 On holiday I don't like lying on the beach, I like to be <u>doing things</u>.

8 The response I got from trying to speak the language was really <u>positive and hopeful</u>.

9 I don't like trips to always be <u>the same</u>, I like a few surprises, too.

10 I thought my last holiday was really <u>fun</u>.

Listening Part 1

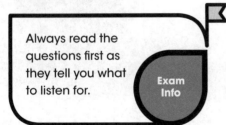

Always read the questions first as they tell you what to listen for.

Exam Info

04 You hear people talking in eight different situations. For questions 1–8, choose the best answer (A, B or C).

1 You overhear a tourist talking about their journey. How does the tourist feel?
   A annoyed because the journey took so long
   B happy because the journey was interesting
   C not bothered by the long journey

2 You overhear a mother and son trying to choose a holiday. Which of the following is a priority for the son?
   A being near a busy place
   B not extending the journey time
   C having a big pool

3 You hear a boy talking to the receptionist in a hotel. When is the boy sure he last saw his watch?
   A He can't remember.
   B When he had finished dinner.
   C In the hotel lobby.

4 You hear the following announcement at an airport. Where should passengers go to get their food token?
   A any of the cafés in the departure lounge
   B the information desk
   C Gate 10

5 You hear a teenage girl telling her mum about her recent holiday. The best thing about the holiday was
   A the weather.
   B making Italian friends.
   C being shown the best places to eat and visit.

6 You overhear two school friends discussing the weather forecast. The girl feels
   A confused.
   B disappointed.
   C shocked.

7 You hear a tour guide giving information to a group of tourists. What will happen if anyone is late?
   A The bus will still leave at 13.00.
   B They will be left behind.
   C They could miss an appointment.

8 You overhear a woman making a complaint to the hotel manager. What does the woman want the manager to do?
   A give her a better room
   B fix something in her room
   C give her a full refund

Reading and Use of English Part 3

For questions 1–8, read the text below. Use the word given in capitals at the end of some of the lines to form a word that fits the gap in the same line. There is an example at the beginning (0).

One of the most **(0)** ....attractive.... destinations for any family has to be Orlando, Florida. This is because the range of theme parks on offer there is	**ATTRACT**
quite **(1)** .... Not only can you visit Disney World, but there are also	**SPECTACLE**
many other **(2)** .... places to see. Sea World and Universal Studios	**MEMORY**
are also **(3)** .... My favourite attraction has to be Universal Studios	**FASCINATE**
because it gives visitors a look behind the scenes at how some of their films	
are made. There are also lots of **(4)** .... rides at these places, but I	**THRILL**
am not really interested in those as I am quite **(5)** .... of heights. The	**FRIGHT**
firework display at the Epcot Centre is also really **(6)** .... and not to	**IMPRESS**
be missed! Try to go out of peak season in order to avoid the **(7)**	**MASS**
queues. Other than that, the place just offers **(8)** .... fun for the	**END**
family, especially those with young children.	

4 Food, glorious food

Grammar

so, such, too, enough, little, few

1 Complete the sentences with one of the following: *so, such, too, enough, little, few*

1 This dinner is ....so.......... tasty, please make it again!
2 Unfortunately, we don't have .... milk to have cereal this morning.
3 I have only tried a .... organic foods.
4 This dish needs a .... more sauce.
5 We had .... a good meal at that restaurant. I would definitely recommend it.
6 Fortunately, the recipe was .... easy and there were only a few steps to follow.
7 My brother has .... interest in learning how to cook.
8 The curry was just .... spicy for me; I would have preferred a milder one.
9 My starter was fine, but I would have liked a .... more garlic.
10 I only know a .... people who have eaten snails.

2 Some of these sentences contain mistakes. Correct the mistakes you find and put a tick (✓) next to the sentences which are correct.

1 Admittedly, I don't eat enough fruit and vegetables.
.....✓.....
2 There just isn't too flavour in this dish. ....
3 There is just so much to prepare for the buffet. ....
4 We don't have such money at the moment, so that restaurant is out of our budget. ....
5 The bread wasn't enough fresh to serve to customers. ....
6 For breakfast I like to eat yoghurt with a little raspberries and blueberries. ....
7 Eating a little chocolate on occasion isn't to unhealthy. ....
8 There are so many ingredients in this recipe, I may have to go to the shops. ....
9 I sometimes like to cook for a little of my friends. ....
10 You shouldn't eat too many processed foods. ....

Vocabulary

Food and diet

1 Circle the most suitable word.

1 Meat, cheese and fish are good *providers / sources* of protein.
2 Eating a(n) *equal / balanced* diet is important for people of all ages.
3 *Vegans / Vegetarians* don't eat meat, but they can eat other animal products such as milk.
4 After my meal I felt so *full / complete*, I couldn't eat another thing!
5 Lemons can taste very *sweet / bitter* on their own.
6 I gave the waiter a *payment / tip* at the end of the meal for the excellent service.
7 I like to *try / experiment* with different ingredients when I am cooking.
8 Nuts can *cause / make* a severe allergic reaction for some people.
9 Currently, my *food / diet* isn't very good because I am eating too much fast food.
10 The restaurant served very big *shares / portions* of food.

2 Complete the following sentences with one of the words in italics from Exercise 1.

1 I can't eat grapefruit for breakfast, it is too ....
2 Now I am older, I can only eat small .... of food.
3 .... can maintain a balanced diet without eating meat.
4 Overeating and lack of exercise can easily .... obesity.
5 At dinner I can't eat a lot; I get .... very easily.
6 My parents always make sure that I have a healthy ....
7 You don't have to .... here, the service is included in the bill.
8 Milk is a good .... of calcium.

Writing Part 2
A Review

Tom, 11, has written a review of his favourite restaurant for the school magazine. Imagine you are the editor and correct the errors which have been underlined.

My favourite **(1)** restaraunt is called Pier Luigi's and it is located in the centre of town. It is an Italian restaurant and **(2)** we went there since I was five. Of course,when I was that age I did not appreciate the food **(3)** as so as I do now. Now I am older, I really look forward to eating at this restaurant with my family, and we often go on special **(4)** ocasions. Not only is the food superb, but the atmosphere is also great.

For starters there is a wide range of **(5)** plates to choose from, but we usually order the tomato garlic bread to share. For the main course we each order **(6)** are own. My brother always has the steak, I have the lasagne and my parents have pizza. All of these **(7)** foods are very tasty and I would **(8)** reccomend you try all of them.

The **(9)** service are also excellent. In fact, over the years **(10)** we are becoming very friendly with a waiter there, and that is one of the reasons we keep going back!

Corrections

1 .... restaurant ....
2 ....
3 ....
4 ....
5 ....
6 ....
7 ....
8 ....
9 ....
10 ....

Reading and Use of English Part 4

Make sure you use the word given in capital letters without changing it. Then check that you have written between two and five words.

Exam Info

For questions 1–6, complete the second sentence so that it has a similar meaning to the first sentence, using the word given. Do not change the word given. You must use between two and five words, including the word given. Here is an example (0).

Example:

0   I ate out more in the past than I do now.
   USED
   I don't eat out .... as much as I used to ....

1   The waiter gave me some advice on what to order for my main course.
   RECOMMEND
   My main course .... by the waiter.

2   'You need to cook this chicken for longer,' said Berty.
   ENOUGH
   'This chicken hasn't
   .... ,' said Berty.

3   I don't know many good recipes.
   FEW
   I only .... recipes.

4   'Maybe the dish was too spicy,' said Jane.
   MILD
   'Perhaps the dish .... ,' said Jane.

5   It is important to eat healthily.
   DIET
   Having .... is of great importance.

6   James had baked an elaborate cake for the celebration.
   MADE
   An elaborate cake .... for the celebration.

Listening Part 2

 You will hear an interview with Ava Brown, a recent winner of a junior cooking show. For questions 1–10, complete the sentences with a word or short phrase.

Before you listen, read the questions and think about the kind of word or words which might fit each gap.

Exam Info

WINNING A COOKING COMPETITION

Ava's love of cooking came from her family who are **(1)** .... about food.

Ava first learnt how to cook Indian dishes because her grandmother **(2)** .... in Goa.

Learning the art of Indian cooking meant that she was good at **(3)** .... flavours in her dishes.

People were **(4)** .... when they tried her cooking.

She had different feelings about being accepted onto the show. On the one hand she felt nervous, yet on the other, she was **(5)** ....

Despite any initial worries she had about being on TV, in the end she decided to
(6) ....

Ava admits that she found the competition difficult at times and she often found herself wanting to
(7) ....

One of the biggest challenges for Ava was managing her school work and the production
(8) ....

She was often asked to perform **(9)** .... and cook within a limited amount of time.

Nevertheless, Ava enjoyed being in the competition because she made friends and learnt some new
(10) .... which will help her to become a better chef.

Reading and Use of English Part 3

For questions 1–8, read the text below. Use the word given in capitals at the end of some of the lines to form a word that fits in the gap in the same line. There is an example at the beginning (0).

Celebrity chef transforms school meals

Jamie Oliver, the celebrity chef, is much more than a media
(0) _____ personality _____ and he has also done a great deal to improve the quality of   **PERSONAL**
school meals in the UK. He began his fight to transform school lunches when he became
(1) _____ about the amount of junk food   **HAPPY**
(2) _____ served to kids at school. Further to this, rates of overeating had   **BE**
also (3) _____ and this caused Jamie to take action.   **INCREASE**

The chef started his campaign by meeting with the prime minister to present the
(4) _____ that the government had a duty to provide healthy and well-   **ARGUE**
balanced meals in all schools. He stated that (5) _____ better food in the   **PROVIDE**
school canteen would improve students' (6) _____ , mood, health, growth   **CONCENTRATE**
and behaviour.

Five years later, school meals in the UK have changed (7) _____ as a result   **CONSIDERABLE**
of Jamie's actions. Although initially the scheme was met with some doubt, it is now viewed
by most with admiration. Schools are now able to report an (8) _____ in   **IMPROVE**
pupils' test results and a decrease in the number of students absent from school.

Grammar

Zero, first and second conditionals

Complete each sentence with the correct tense of the verb in brackets.

1 If his parents had the money, he ......*would go*...... (go) on the school trip.

2 If she .... (study) hard enough, she will do well in her exams.

3 Don't enrol on the course unless you .... (have) the time to complete it.

4 If I pass all of my exams, my parents .... (buy) me a car.

5 You .... (not find) your homework difficult if you listened more in class.

6 If we are absent from school, the teachers .... (want) to know why.

7 Her parents .... (be) much happier if she was better behaved at school.

8 If I can drop a subject, I .... (choose) history.

9 If my parents .... (allow) it, I would study abroad.

10 If I don't study hard, I .... (not get) the qualifications I need.

Vocabulary

Words often confused

1 These sentences contain incorrect words. Use the words in the box below to help you correct them.

> seem   remind   matter   lend   hope
> ~~accept~~   teach   revise

1 He ~~excepted~~ the fact that he wasn't very good at studying languages. ....*accepted*....

2 She spent all day reviewing before the test. ....

3 I am always asking my classmates to borrow me a pen.
....

4 During his long career as a teacher, he had learnt many students.
....

5 My teacher always remembers me of someone on the television. ....

6 The teacher didn't look to mind that we couldn't finish everything. ....

7 I wish that I do well in my exams this summer. ....

8 My parents say it doesn't mind how I do in tests, just as long as I do my best. ....

Phrasal verbs

2 Replace each underlined word or phrase with a phrasal verb from the box. Put it in the correct tense.

> get over   sort out   run out   turn out
> try out   carry out   ~~find out~~

Last week my school organised a work experience week, so we could all **(1)** <u>discover</u> .....*find out*..... what it would be like in the world of work. It was really interesting and we all **(2)** <u>experienced</u> .... different types of job depending on our interests. My experience was working in the office of a local graphic design company. At the beginning of the week I was really nervous, but luckily I soon **(3)** <u>recover</u> ....this feeling when I realised how friendly everyone was. I was only asked to **(4)** <u>do</u> .... basic tasks, such as make coffee or **(5)** <u>organise</u> .... the mail, but it was still enjoyable. On the last day, I went into town with the receptionist, as we had **(6)** <u>used up</u> all .... of the office supplies. Overall, I think the week **(7)** <u>happened</u> .... to be successful. It certainly made a change from being at school!

Study words

3 Complete the sentences below with the words from the box.

> analyse   fees   capable   qualifications   assess
> research   discipline   theory   ~~terms~~   compulsory

1   He didn't understand some mathematical .... *terms* .... , so he had to use the dictionary.
2   In the UK, education is .... until you are sixteen.
3   State schools are free, but for private schools you have to pay ....
4   The teacher often found it difficult to .... his students when they misbehaved.
5   He studied hard at school, in order to get good ....
6   Students have to do a lot of .... for their final project.
7   In science we can test a .... by carrying out different experiments.
8   The students have to .... the results of the experiment to get a good mark.
9   Teachers use the test result to .... the ability of their students.
10   His teachers said he was a very .... student, when he tried.

Word formation – suffixes

4 Use the following suffixes to change the verbs in the box into nouns:
-ation, *-ence*, *-ment*, or *-ance*. Write them in the correct column.

> ~~prefer~~   assist   concentrate   dominate   encourage   guide   ignore   tolerate
> equip   hesitate   refer   involve   require   agree   argue   independent

-ation	-ence	-ment	-ance
	preference		

5 Complete these sentences with the appropriate nouns from the table. A plural form might be needed.

1   In order to be accepted onto the course he needed to fulfil all the entry ....
2   In our class today we discussed the .... for and against being vegetarian.
3   We use a lot of .... during our PE lessons, which we must put away afterwards.
4   He often lacks .... during class and just looks out of the window.
5   The student denied any .... in the incident which took place.
6   Our school encourages an attitude of .... towards all people.
7   Arts or science – what's your .... ?
8   The lab assistants can provide .... on how to use the science equipment.

5

You are going to read an article about some of the most successful school systems around the world. Choose from the sentences A–G the one which fits each gap (1–6). There is one extra sentence which you do not need to use.

When you have chosen a sentence for each gap, read the text before and after the gap again to check your answers.

Exam Info

Studying around the world

Japan, Switzerland and Finland are just some of the education systems which have been ranked as the best in the world by a recent study. Although all three of these countries have produced some very effective results in education, interestingly, they are also very different in approach. In the following article we will look at just how these systems operate.

The Japanese education system is compulsory for nine years: students start their school life at six and are allowed to leave by the age of fifteen, after completing both elementary and junior high school. **1** Most schools have three terms and the school year starts in April and finishes at the end of March. For junior high school pupils, the school day starts at 8.45 a.m. and finishes at 3.15 p.m., although most students also attend after-school clubs. Lunch is not served in a canteen but eaten in the classroom with the teacher. The number of students in one class is usually under forty. **2** As

well as studying the usual subjects, such as maths and science, pupils also learn the traditional arts, like 'shodo' and 'haiku'. Shodo involves writing with a brush and ink, whereas haiku is a form of poetry developed in Japan about four hundred years ago. Generally, there is a high level of discipline in Japanese schools and students very rarely skip lessons or are disrespectful to teachers.

Switzerland also has a well-respected education system. In Switzerland most pupils attend state schools, which they start when they are either four or six. **3** Lessons are taught in different languages depending on the region the school is in; students are most commonly taught in either French, German or Italian. Aside from this, pupils are also required to learn one of the other official Swiss languages, as well as English. Swiss children start the day at 8.30 a.m. and then have a break at 11.30 a.m. until 1.30 p.m., when they resume until 4.00 p.m. Primary schools also usually have shorter days than secondary schools, and are closed one day or afternoon a week. After their compulsory education is complete, at the age of fifteen or sixteen, Swiss students are given several options: they can either receive training in a particular job or profession or complete a preparation course for university. **4**

Lastly, the Finnish school system is probably the most talked about education system in the world. **5** Finnish students only start school when they are seven and the school day starts between 8 and 9 a.m. and finishes between 1 and 2 p.m. During this time, there is a great deal of emphasis on free time and play and by law, teachers must give students a fifteen-minute break for every forty-five minutes of instruction. There is also little emphasis on pupils doing homework or being tested. **6** Pupils are not separated by ability and the average class size is about twenty. Finnish students are encouraged to feel a sense of belonging to their school, class and class teacher. For example, pupils address their teachers by their first name and they eat lunch together.

A Most students choose the work-related route and gain experience in a company.	**E** However, in the past this was much higher, due to the rapid growth in population.
B This is because it provides first-rate results, as well as being very unusual.	**F** Surprisingly, only five per cent of students attend private schools.
C Therefore, the majority of students achieve good grades.	**G** This is rarely the case however, and over 95 per cent of students choose to continue their education.
D In fact, students are only given one formal assessment in their entire school life.	

Listening Part 3

(06) You will hear five short extracts in which British teenagers are talking about how they like to study. For questions 1–5, choose from the list (A–H). Use the letters only once. There are three extra letters which you do not need to use.

A I have parents who disapprove of my study method.

B I like the fact that my study method is very flexible.

C I study best when I am under pressure.

D I need to study all night in order to do well.

E I don't always keep accurate notes.

F I study best using visual notes.

G I have only just discovered the best way to study.

H I always perform well in tests because I am mentally prepared.

Speaker 1		1
Speaker 2		2
Speaker 3		3
Speaker 4		4
Speaker 5		5

Reading and Use of English Part 3

For questions 1–8, read the text below. Use the word given in capitals at the end of some of the lines to form a word that fits in the gap in the same line. There is an example at the beginning (0).

> When you have finished, always check that you have spelt your answers correctly.
>
> **Exam Info**

Having a Mentor

When I first arrived at my new school they gave me a mentor, which my form tutor explained to me was a more **(0)** ...... *experienced* ...... student who could give me help and **(1)** .... when I needed it. **(2)** .... , when we met I really liked him and felt **(3)** .... by the fact that I knew someone in the school, other than the teachers, who I could talk to. In the beginning, we used to meet at least once a week and **(4)** .... we would just chat about how I was feeling. During my first term I did experience a few **(5)** .... and he was really helpful and gave me the **(6)** .... I needed to overcome these problems. I don't really see him much anymore, as I am into my third term and I feel quite settled now. **(7)** .... , I found having a mentor really **(8)** .... and I would definitely recommend it to other students.

EXPERIENCE
GUIDE
FORTUNE

ENCOURAGE

GENERAL

DIFFICULT
CONFIDENT

NEVER
BENEFIT

6 My first job

Grammar

Articles

1 Complete each gap with *a*, *the* or *–*.

THE SKI SLOPES WERE MY OFFICE!

One of the very first jobs I had was working as
(1) ...._a_........ ski instructor in the French Alps. I started
learning how to ski when I was **(2)** .... child, so by
(3) .... time I was **(4)** .... teenager, I had
become quite **(5)** .... capable skier. I had also met
many young instructors who had done this role before going
to **(6)** .... university, and so I became inspired to do
the same! After completing my initial training and gaining
(7) .... necessary qualifications, I was hired by
(8) .... large ski company who gave me
(9) .... position in Chamonix, **(10)** ....
very popular ski resort in **(11)** .... France. Overall, I
have very fond memories of this experience and I made some
great friends. **(12)** .... job wasn't always perfect – I
had several demanding clients and **(13)** .... pay
wasn't great, but I loved working outdoors and
(14) .... interacting with **(15)** .... people
all **(16)** .... day.

Countable and uncountable nouns

2 Complete each sentence with a word from the box. You
don't need to use all the words but you will need to
make some of them plural.

> company   responsibility   work   job   bonus
> suggestion   ~~research~~   salary   hour   staff
> money   information   food

1 My ideal job would be carrying out lots of
........_research_........ on rare diseases.

2 My dad really likes his job, but he has to work long
hours because he has so much .... to do.

3 When I'm older I'd like to be a teacher, but I think that
they have to remember a lot of ....

4 When you first get a job, the .... will
probably be low, so don't be too disappointed.

5 Every December .... were awarded to
employees, based on their performance during the
year.

6 The company was doing really well, so eventually it
needed to hire new ....

7 Her first job was working in a kitchen, where she
helped prepare all the .... for the guests.

8 In the meeting she made many good ....
which her colleagues agreed with.

9 Nowadays people often work for several ....
throughout their career.

10 She took the job because of the flexible working
....

Vocabulary

Adjective collocations with *job* and *work*

1 For each sentence, choose a word from the box. Then
circle *job* or *work* in each sentence.

> temporary   voluntary   summer   applying for
> well-paid   part-time

1 I still have to go to college on Mondays, Wednesdays
and Fridays, so I only want a .... *job* / *work*.

2 He really needed to spend more time .... *job*
/ *work*.

3 She only wanted a .... *job* / *work*, as she was
moving to London in six months, and there was no
point looking for a permanent position.

4 When school finishes the weather will be good, but I
won't go on holiday, I'll find a .... *job* / *work*.

5 She wanted to get a .... *job* / *work* so she
could afford a new car.

6 I don't get paid for it, but I really enjoy my
.... *job* / *work*, as I like to help the local
community.

Words often confused

2 Six of the sentences below contain an incorrect word. Correct them and put a tick (✓) next to the sentences which are correct.

1 She was quite successful and owned a local dental ~~practise~~. *practice*

2 He was very happy to retire at sixty-five. ✓

3 The manager's role was to insure the company made a profit. ....

4 Fortunately, the company gave their staff regular brakes. ....

5 He is a very loyal employee who has been with this company for years. ....

6 She found be self-employed very challenging. ....

7 Employees were advice that there would be changes in the New Year. ....

8 He was not aloud to use his mobile during work hours. ....

Writing Part 2
A letter

1 Read the exam question below. Then complete each gap in the reply with a linking word or phrase from the box.

THEME PARK RANGER WANTED
(summer work)

Theme park ranger wanted for the summer holidays

- **Do you like working with people?**
- **Are you enthusiastic and flexible?**

Our theme park is looking for someone to operate the rides and serve people food from our stalls during July and August.

No experience is required as full training is provided.

Write your letter of application saying:
- Why you want the job
- Why you are a suitable candidate.

Write 140–190 words in an appropriate style.

---

so	candidate	apply	opportunity	reference
	~~Sir~~	consideration	Furthermore	

Dear (1) ....*Sir*....... or Madam,

I am writing to (2) .... for a position at your theme park this summer, as recently advertised on your website. I am a hard-working Year 11 student and I would love the (3) .... to work for your company this summer.

I live very close to your fantastic theme park, and I have been a regular visitor there since I was a small child. I know the place very well and this would make me a good (4) .... for the position. I also understand that the role of park ranger is varied, (5) .... I am very willing to be flexible and do whatever is required.

(6) ...., as you can see from my CV, I already have some work experience in a café. As well as preparing and serving food, my responsibilities included handling money and dealing with customers.

Thank you for your (7) .... and I look forward to hearing from you soon. I enclose a (8) .... from my previous employer.

Yours faithfully,

Tom Baker

2 Answer these questions.

1 Why does Tom think he is suitable for the role?

2 What suitable skills does Tom have for the position?

3 Match the following functions to each paragraph:

Explain why you would like the job.
Paragraph ....

State any previous experience that you have.
Paragraph ....

Introduce yourself and state the position you are applying for.
Paragraph ....

Listening Part 1

07 **You will hear people talking in eight different situations. For questions 1–8, choose the best answer (A, B or C).**

1 You hear a man giving career advice to a group of teenagers. How does he feel about the advice he was given when he was young?
   A happy that he was helped
   B happy that he was advised to do something he enjoyed
   C happy that he was independent in his choice of career

2 You hear a girl being interviewed for a part-time job at a café. What does the woman think about the girl?
   A She likes her approach.
   B She doesn't have enough experience.
   C She is very polite.

3 You hear a teacher talking to his students about their work experience week. He is
   A making preparations.
   B giving advice.
   C making an offer.

4 You hear a teenager interviewing a man about his job. What is the man's job?
   A a police officer
   B a doctor
   C a firefighter

5 You hear two teenagers talking about their summer job working at an ice cream stall.
   Why does the girl not want the boy to go to the shop?
   A It isn't essential.
   B There are many people waiting to be served.
   C They are getting more stock tomorrow.

6 You hear a man leave a message on an answering machine. Which candidate was chosen for the job originally advertised?
   A someone who performed better at the interview
   B someone already working for the company
   C someone with better qualifications

7 You hear a teenage girl talking to her father about her first day at a new job. How does she feel?
   A frustrated
   B hopeful
   C patient

8 You hear a teenage boy talking to his boss. When has his boss agreed to give him time off?
   A Saturday afternoon
   B the weekend
   C Saturday morning

Reading and Use of English Part 7

You are going to read an article about being a vet. For questions 1–10, choose from the people (A–D). The people may be chosen more than once.

Which person says

they need to think about protecting their staff?	1
they can feel sad if they are not able to treat a client?	2
they grew up in the countryside?	3
they feel lucky to be a vet?	4
they are often surprised by how grateful clients can be?	5
they sometimes feel their job is demanding?	6
they are not concerned by the negative aspects of their job?	7
they think it is important to be flexible about how your career will progress?	8
they think being a vet can be a very varied profession?	9
they help other vets acquire the skills they need?	10

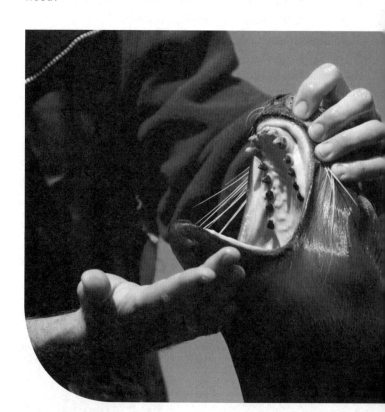

LIFE AS A VET

A Amy

From an early age I knew I wanted to be a farm vet. I come from a rural area and a farming background, so the decision to go to vet school came as no surprise to anyone. However, after graduating something quite unexpected happened, and my career went in a completely different direction. But, this has turned out to be a good thing and now I realise you shouldn't have fixed ideas when you first start working. I am still a vet, but I don't work on a farm at all. Instead, I work for a small animal practice and I really love my work. The best thing about my job is the bond you develop with the pets and their owners. Pets are a big part of family life for many people, and therefore, it is so important that they receive the correct care and treatment when they need it. The level of appreciation I get for my work sometimes is just amazing. Of course, the negative side to that, is that when you are unable to help, it can also be very upsetting, for me and for my clients. My advice to anyone wanting to be a vet would be to keep an open mind!

B Toby

When I first applied to vet school I knew I wanted to work on a farm, with sheep. Currently, I am working on a large farm, but mostly with cattle. I find my job really fascinating and every day brings a new challenge. The best thing about my role is that I get to work outdoors all day and meet other people who like working with farm animals. The only disadvantage to the job is that it can be lonely when I have to go out and the road and it is always quite stressful. This doesn't bother me though, because I get on well with my colleagues and my employer. My goal for the future is to publish an article in the *Veterinary Times*.

C Rosy

I work part-time for a small animal practice in my local town and I also give some talks at schools in the area. I have always been fascinated by animals and so I feel really fortunate to have the career I do. My favourite thing about being a vet is that every day there is a new problem to solve. The worst thing is accepting that sometimes you don't have the answer. Still, there are so many different jobs you can have as a vet; it is such an exciting profession. When I was younger, I even travelled with the job and spent some time at a practice in South Africa.

D Ben

Since finishing vet school, I have been working in a zoo, taking care of wild animal health. Generally, I deal with any problems that arise and make sure that everything possible is done to prevent the animals from getting sick. For example, we give them X-rays, take blood samples and even check their teeth. I also do some work with training other vets and take part in conservation projects. These projects help reintroduce some species back into the wild. The best thing about my job is that it is very stimulating, and the animals are incredible. The hardest aspect of my job is having to make tough decisions, which will ensure the animal's health and the team's safety. The best advice I can give to anyone wanting this type of role, would be to get involved in voluntary wildlife work.

7 High adventure

Grammar

Infinitive and verb + -ing

1 Complete the sentences with the correct form of the verb in brackets (the infinitive or *-ing* form). In some of the sentences, both are correct.

1 I like .... (cycle) more than any other sport.

2 Don't forget .... (pack) plenty of food and water for the expedition.

3 I intend .... (learn) some new sports next year.

4 I am doing this race for charity, so I promise .... (finish) it.

5 I can't stand .... (run); I prefer swimming.

6 I am not a big fan of extreme sports, such as .... (jump) out of planes.

7 I fancy .... (try) something new this weekend. What do you think?

8 I don't mind .... (climb), as long as we have the right equipment.

9 Halfway through the course I wanted to give up, but my friend persuaded me .... (continue).

10 My favourite activity when we go on holiday is .... (surf).

11 I learnt how .... (ski) from a very young age.

12 I plan .... (go) trekking next summer.

2 Complete the sentences with the correct form of a verb from the box.

require	~~report~~	reach	provide	expect
raise	remain	avoid		

1 It was .....*reported*..... that the weather wasn't suitable for the event to go ahead.

2 Due to the hot weather, two hours into the race there were only a few participants .... , although all of them managed to reach the finishing line.

3 You are .... to be over 18 or you will not be allowed on this training course.

4 She managed to .... for the next rock on the climbing wall.

5 He was taking part in the jump in order to .... money for charity.

6 I really didn't .... to enjoy that bungee jump, but it was actually thrilling.

7 You don't need to take anything with you, as the venue .... all the equipment you need.

8 In order to .... disappointment, you must book your adventure holiday early.

Vocabulary

Phrasal verbs and expressions with *take*

1 Complete the sentences using the correct form of one of the expressions from the box.

take something for granted	take on	take off
take over	take back	take in

1 I .... all of the bad things that I said, white water rafting is amazing.

2 After a while, the instructor had to .... because I was finding it difficult to steer.

3 I am so lucky that I can try all these new activities, sometimes I ....

4 I would like to get my sailing qualifications, but I don't want to .... too much work.

5 The view was so breathtaking, it was almost difficult to ....

6 I never thought this activity would .... , but people seem to love it.

2 Look at the phrasal verbs and their definitions. Then complete the sentences with the correct verb in the correct form.

take sb on	to compete against someone
take up	to use an amount of time or space
be taken in	to be deceived by someone
take sb out	to go somewhere with someone and pay for them
take down	to remove something that is on a wall or something that is temporary
take to sb / sthg	to start to like someone or something

1 I can't believe she lied about doing a parachute jump, I was completely ....

2 John challenged me to a go-karting race and I am going to .... at the weekend.

3 After the race my parents .... for a meal to celebrate.

4 I really .... diving on holiday, I will definitely do it again.

5 We .... the tent, because the weather was just awful.

6 I don't think we can pack all that equipment, it .... too much room in the car.

Verb collocations with sporting activities

3 Circle the correct word.

1 Every Saturday, I like *playing / doing* karate at my local sports centre.

2 I have never *played / done* squash before.

3 On holiday I really enjoy *doing / going* swimming in the sea.

4 At school we often *go / do* gymnastics.

5 I love *seeing / watching* the tennis at Wimbledon.

6 I couldn't *hear / listen* the score, because there was too much noise.

Writing Part 2
A review

4 Find ten spelling mistakes in this review. The first one has been done for you.

Review of a FAMILY FUN MUD RUN

Last weekend I tried something new and exciting with my family. We went on a family mud run and it was brilliant. ~~Basicaly~~ *Basically*, it is an obstacle course which is three kilometres long and you get covered in mud while doing it.

It is great because the whole experience is just for fun. Throughout the day we did lots of jumping, crawling, climbing and runing. You don't have to be really fit to do it though, and some people just walked round and still had a good time. There were also other activities on ofer at the site, such as a bouncy castle, boot throwing and even a disco. You could also eat there and a fitness instructer did a warm up sesion before the event started.

The only bad thing about the venue was that there were no showers there to wash all the mud of afterwards. They did have some washing facilties, but it was difficult to get completly clean. I would definetely recomend the experience though, but not to anyone who doesn't like mud!

Listening Part 2

08 You will hear part of an interview with Vanessa White, a climbing expert. For questions 1–10, complete the sentences with a word or a short phrase.

CLIMBING

Vanessa is pleased that she is viewed as an
(1) .... to new climbers.

She says that the potential which very young climbers are showing these days is **(2)** ....

She enjoys climbing so much because it tests her body as well as her **(3)** .... strength.

When she started climbing, Vanessa was very competitive and winning became an **(4)** ....

Currently Vanessa feels less **(5)** ....
when she climbs because she already feels successful.

Vanessa suggests that practising with expert climbers can be **(6)** ....

She also states that when you first start to climb it can take some time to increase your level of
(7) ....

You also need the right footwear as this can affect your ability to **(8)** .... properly.

One climbing route which she found difficult, eventually became an **(9)** .... for her.

Despite her finding this particular climb difficult, she managed to keep her **(10)** ....

Reading and Use of English Part 2

For questions 1–8, read the text below and think of the word which best fits each gap. Use only one word in each gap. There is an example at the beginning (0).

Extreme Sports

Extreme sports are sports **(0)** ....*which*.... are known to be of high risk or speed, such as snowboarding, skydiving or freestyle skiing. These sports are all about **(1)** .... thrill of it. Some people do them just **(2)** .... fun, while others really test the limits of what is humanly possible. It first **(3)** .... popular in the 1990's and appeals mostly to the younger generation. The most well-known extreme sports competition began **(4)** .... the USA in 1995, and is called the 'X Games'. These games are held annually, **(5)** .... in the summer and winter, in order to cater **(6)** .... all the major extreme sports. People who compete in such events do it mainly for the adrenaline rush that potential danger provides. However, just **(7)** .... the Olympics, there are many other incentives, and the competition awards medals and a cash prize to those **(8)** .... are successful. Some competitors also become famous, as every X Games is televised around the world.

Reread the whole text when you have finished to make sure the words you have written make sense.

Exam Info

Reading and Use of English Part 1

For questions 1–8, read the text below and decide which answer (A, B, C or D) best fits each gap. There is an example at the beginning (0).

Some questions test words which are part of fixed expressions.

Exam Info

Example:

0   A jumping   **B** falling   Ⓒ launching   **D** pulling

Bungee Jumping

Bungee jumping is an extreme sport which involves **(0)** .... yourself off a great height, whilst still **(1)** .... to a long elastic cord, which is attached to your ankle. Bungee jumping usually takes place from bridges, cliffs or cranes, and the jumper is given the **(2)** .... of falling until they are pulled back by the cord. **(3)** .... it looking very dangerous, it actually has an excellent **(4)** .... record, as most providers are managed by trained and experienced professionals.

The first commercial jump took place in the mid-1980s in New Zealand and was **(5)** .... by a man named AJ Hackett. Hackett attempted his first amateur jump in 1986 from the Upper Harbour bridge in Auckland. Since then, he has **(6)** .... promoted the sport and it has now been experienced by millions **(7)** .... In 1987 he even did a jump off the Eiffel Tower in order to draw **(8)** .... to the sport.

1	**A**	combined	**B**	united	**C**	connected	**D**	holding
2	**A**	emotion	**B**	awareness	**C**	thought	**D**	sensation
3	**A**	Despite	**B**	Although	**C**	Even though	**D**	However
4	**A**	safety	**B**	security	**C**	safeness	**D**	maintenance
5	**A**	structured	**B**	created	**C**	made	**D**	organised
6	**A**	urgently	**B**	severely	**C**	roughly	**D**	actively
7	**A**	international	**B**	worldwide	**C**	people	**D**	global
8	**A**	recognition	**B**	consideration	**C**	attention	**D**	notice

Grammar
Reported speech

1 After watching the latest film release, a group of school friends were asked for their opinion by a local reporter. Write the words each person actually said.

1 Fin said the film was better than he had expected it to be.

2 Charlotte told the reporter that she thought the acting was really good.

3 Jacob said it was so good that he would watch it again.

4 Chloe said that she had preferred reading the book.

5 Grace said that she had been confused by the plot.

6 Tom told the reporter that the ending had been disappointing.

1 Fin: _'the film was better than I expected it to be.'_

2 Charlotte: ....

3 Jacob: ....

4 Chloe: ....

5 Grace: ....

6 Tom: ....

Reporting verbs

2 Match what the people said (A–G) with a reporting verb from the box.

> invite   accuse   warn   recommend   boast
> deny   ~~insist~~

A I am telling the truth

..........._insist_...........

B I'm going to be the star of the show!

....

C He went to the theatre without paying for a ticket!

....

D She can come to the play with me if you like.

....

E I don't know anything about the prop being stolen.

....

F If he doesn't learn his lines, he won't be performing!

....

G Gary, you should go and see this film!

....

3 Now report what the people in Exercise 2 said.

1 Susan accused
him of going to the theatre without paying for a ticket.

2 Anna boasted that
....

3 Peter warned him that
....

4 Lisa denied any knowledge that
....

5 Stephen recommended that
....

6 Isobel invited her
....

7 Joe insisted that
....

Vocabulary
Entertainment

1 Put the words in the box in the correct column in the table.

> documentary   scene   ~~performer~~   stage
> producer   venue   audience   series   spectator
> comedian   performance   director   location
> set   cast   thrillers   box office   public
> recording studio

People	Place	Other
performer		

2 Complete the following sentences with words from the table.

1 This ....venue........... was the perfect location for the concert.

2 Every time I see this .... she gets funnier.

3 Tonight's .... was spectacular, the cast really did a good job.

4 The final .... of the film was really moving.

5 I hope they make another ...., I really enjoyed this one.

6 I found this .... on her life story really fascinating and informative.

7 We need to collect our tickets from the .... before watching the performance.

8 My favourite films are ...., because they keep you on the edge of your seat.

9 She met a lot of famous actors on the .... of the film when she visited Hollywood.

10 After the final performance, the director threw a party for the entire ....

Verb collocations with *ambition, career, experience* and *job*

3 Choose the correct word, A–D, for each gap.

1 If you want to be an actor, you should ....*gain*......... some work experience by working in a theatre.

   A gain   **B** achieve   **C** provide   **D** increase

2 After years of performing in small venues, she finally .... her ambition of singing in front of a large audience.

   A completed   **B** produced   **C** achieved   **D** acquired

3 In order to .... his modelling career he had to move to the city.

   A chase   **B** go after   **C** attempt   **D** pursue

4 I was told that I wasn't .... for the job, because I didn't have enough experience.

   A useful   **B** suitable   **C** applicable
   D convenient

5 It is a real shame that this one incident has .... his career.

   A wasted   **B** failed   **C** ruined   **D** deleted

Listening Part 3

🎧 09 You will hear five short extracts in which people are talking about a concert they have been to. For questions 1–5, choose from the list (A–H) what each person thinks about the concert. Use the letters only once. There are three extra letters which you do not need to use.

A There wasn't enough happening on stage.

B This act was as good as advertised on television.

C This act has had a long and successful career and is still good.

D The singer's jokes were the best thing about the performance.

E The performance didn't start on time.

F This act used to be entertaining but isn't anymore.

G This act interacted well with fans.

H The performers didn't play enough of their old songs.

Speaker 1		1
Speaker 2		2
Speaker 3		3
Speaker 4		4
Speaker 5		5

Reading and Use of English Part 4

For questions 1–6, complete the second sentence so it has a similar meaning to the first sentence, using the word given. Do not change the word given. You must use between two and five words, including the word given. Here is an example (0).

Example:

0 'I think it would be a good idea if you went to drama school.'
ATTEND

It was recommended ….. *to me that I attend* ….. drama school.

1 'I really want to be a professional singer, mum,' said Jane.
CAREER

Jane revealed to her mum ………………………………… as a professional singer.

2 'I wasn't very happy with the way I performed,' said Sarah.
QUALITY

Sarah complained ……………………………… her performance.

3 'I really would like to pay for your tickets,' said James.
INSISTED

James ……………………………… for our tickets.

4 'The entertainment business won't be easy, you know, Julie,' said Dad.
WARN

Julie's father ……………………………… be hard in the entertainment business.

5 Mary insisted that she could remember her lines, if given another chance.
BEGGED

Mary ……………………………… remember her lines.

6 'Look Anna, I'll definitely return your book,' said Tony.
PROMISED

Tony ……………………………… her book back.

Reading and Use of English Part 6

You are going to read an article about a comedian called Edward Miller. Six sentences have been removed from the article. Choose from the sentences A–G the one which fills each gap (1–6). There is one extra sentence which you do not need to use.

Comedy has always been a big part of Edward Miller's life. He first started telling jokes when he was at school and would always be the one to make his classmates laugh. As you can imagine, this made him very popular with the other students, but not so popular with his teachers. **1** | | According to his parents, it was this experience which gave him the confidence and encouragement he needed to pursue a career in comedy. Edward recalls the first time he attempted stand-up comedy: 'I was so nervous, I thought I was going to be sick. But then the audience started to laugh at my jokes, and the atmosphere was just amazing. I became hooked.'

After finishing school, Edward went to university and continued to follow his dream of becoming a comedian by joining an amateur theatre club. It was here that the youngster really developed his comedic style and talent for performing. **2** | | Edward says that he remembers these university days with a real fondness, although he admits that some of his initial performances didn't always go to plan. 'I remember one night I was in the middle of telling a joke and I just forgot what I was going to say,' he recalls. 'Of course from that moment on, I just lost the audience that night.' **3** | | Fortunately, however, he was persuaded otherwise by one of his close friends at the time.

Currently, Edward is one of the most successful comedians in the country. **4** | | During his first major tour it is estimated that Edward has performed to approximately 600,000 people. For next year, there are already plans in place for him to extend his tour worldwide, performing 64 times in over sixteen countries. What's more, his DVD of the tour has been number one in the best sellers list for the past six months.

When asked about his impressive career, Edward attributes his success to his genuine desire to make people laugh. **5** | | Perhaps the best thing about Edward's brand of comedy, however, is that he isn't offensive or rude to anyone in the process. Most of the time, he is actually just making fun of himself.

6 | | He states, 'If you lose your confidence on stage, your audience will instantly lose confidence in you, and that's when things start to go wrong.' He also adds that you must not be frightened of criticism or a bad performance, as it is these experiences which will make you stronger and more able in the long term.

A Edward states that after this particular experience, he did consider giving up comedy.

B However, it was clear that his ambition was always to be a comedian.

C Edward's advice to anyone wanting to be a comedian is to believe in yourself at all costs.

D 'My comedy is observational – I write about ordinary things that everyone in the audience can understand,' he says.

E When he was just twelve years old he started to take classes at the local comedy club, which were especially designed for young people.

F As well as regularly appearing on radio and television shows he has also spent the year selling out venues nationwide.

G He performed every fortnight to a live and paying audience, and this regular practice was vital in shaping the professional act which we see today.

9 Secrets of the mind

Grammar

Modal verbs to express certainty and possibility

1 Rewrite the sentences in *italics* using a modal verb: *might, may, could, must* or *can't*.

1 Olivia seems happy. *I'm sure she got the job.*
   She ....*must have*........ got the job.

2 Tom is alone whilst his parents are away. *Perhaps he is feeling lonely.*
   He .... feeling lonely.

3 *Sarah is thinking of studying psychology at university. She isn't sure yet.*
   She .... study psychology at university.

4 *Stephen is unable to make a speech in public.* He just gets too nervous.
   Due to his nerves, Stephen .... make good speeches in public.

5 *Michael has the opportunity to go on the trip.* Unfortunately, he is afraid of flying.
   He .... go on the trip, if he wasn't afraid of flying.

6 Let's go to the party and be sociable. *It is possible that we will meet some new friends.*
   Let's go to the party because we .... make some new friends.

7 I wish I had relaxed more today. *I need to make sure I am mentally prepared for the race.*
   I .... prepare myself mentally for tomorrow's race.

8 Tell me what is wrong. *There is a chance I will be able to help.*
   There is a chance I .... be able to help, if you let me know what is wrong.

9 *It is very important that you remain active.* This helps to maintain a healthy mind.
   If you want to maintain a healthy mind, you .... remain active.

10 *It was suggested that Mary was doing too much.* That's why she was so tired.
   It .... be that she was doing too much.

2 Read the paragraph about how the weather can affect people's mood. Circle the correct modal verbs.

SO HOW DOES THE WEATHER AFFECT OUR MOOD?

(1) *Can / May* it really make us depressed or happy? Psychologists have always believed that the weather **(2)** *must / can* have a big impact on how a person feels. In fact, a great deal of research has been carried out on how sunshine, in particular, **(3)** *can / could* make people more positive and less tired. Studies have not only shown that the sun **(4)** *must / can* make us happier, but they have also revealed that it **(5)** *may / must* also affect the way we behave. Apparently, when the sun is out people are more likely to be helpful, generous and even romantic. Although many of these findings **(6)** *can't / must not* be scientifically proven, it **(7)** *could / must* be said that many of us do feel happier when the sun is shining!

Writing Part 2

An article

You see this advertisement in your school magazine.

> Who is the most positive person you know?
>
> What positive things do they say and do?
>
> What positive effect have they had on you and / or other people?

Write your article in 140–190 words.

Read the example and answer the questions.

The most positive person I have ever met is my good friend Sarah. I met her about eight years ago and whenever I am with her she just makes me feel more optimistic about life.

I think one of the key things which makes her a positive person is that she is very grateful for what she has. She doesn't care for material objects a great deal and loves to spend time with her family and friends. She also has lots of different interests and gets excited at the prospect of trying new experiences or activities. Furthermore, I really admire the way she seems to have no fear. She always tells me that I shouldn't be afraid of failure, as it is a natural part of life and eventually these struggles will amount to success.

Perhaps most importantly, Sarah also smiles a lot and takes great pride in her appearance. When I am around her, she always inspires me to be more active and make more of an effort with how I present myself to the world. Sarah has lots of friends and I know they also feel the same way.

1 When you write an article, you should try and think of an interesting heading. Choose the best heading.

A My best friend

B My optimistic friend

C An interesting person

2 Match the paragraphs to what their function is.

A Development of ideas

B Introduction to the topic

C Summary and conclusion

3 Read the article and find the following:

1 a connecting word that means every or any time *(adv)* (Para 1)

2 hoping or believing that good things will happen in the future *(adj)* (Para 1)

3 a very important part of something *(adj)* (Para 2)

4 showing thanks for something *(adj)* (Para 2)

5 in addition *(adj)* (Para 2)

6 to have respect for somebody or something *(verb)* (Para 2)

7 to make somebody feel they want to do something and can do it *(verb)* (Para 3)

Vocabulary

stay, spend and *pass; make, cause* and *have; achieve, carry out* and *devote*

1 Circle the correct verb.

1 Psychologists *spend / pass* a great deal of time trying to understand the mind.

2 When I want to relax, I often like to just *spend / stay* at home.

3 In order to *stay / pass* healthy you must take care of your mind and body.

4 I don't really have anything to do, I am just *passing / spending* the time until my friend arrives.

5 I didn't sleep well at all and I *spent / passed* the whole night worrying.

6 I usually play a game on my phone to *pass / spend* the time.

2 Which verbs in the table collocate with the nouns in the box? Put the nouns in the correct column. Some can go in more than one column.

> a problem   ~~an excuse~~   an exception   a decision
> an argument   a conversation   an accident
> a suggestion   a promise   a comment   a choice
> a complaint   a meeting

make	cause	have
an excuse		

3 Match the two parts of the sentences.

1 She devoted …

2 He really wanted to achieve …

3 Psychologists carry out …

4 Happiness can be achieved …

5 Scientists have carried out …

6 He devotes …

A if you have a more positive approach to life.

B his goals in order to make his parents proud.

C research which suggested that a hug can improve your mood.

D much of her time to people who suffered from loneliness.

E many experiments in order to understand the mind.

F himself mostly to his work, which isn't particularly good for his social life.

1 .... **2** .... **3** ....

4 .... **5** .... **6** ....

Adjectives describing personality

4 Match the adjectives with the definitions.

1	stubborn	**A**	easily upset by the things people say or do
2	honest	**B**	taking care to avoid risks or danger
3	bossy	**C**	sincere and telling the truth
4	cautious	**D**	kind and always thinking about how you can help other people
5	sensitive	**E**	determined not to change your ideas or plans, even if asked to
6	thoughtful	**F**	always telling other people what to do

5 Now choose one adjective from above to describe the people in each photograph.

Listening Part 4

You will hear an interview with a health specialist on the advantages and disadvantages of living in the countryside, rather than in urban areas. For questions 1–7, choose the best answer (A, B or C).

1 Peter Banks states that living in the city
  A may have an impact on your physical health.
  B definitely has an impact on your physical health.
  C may have an impact on your physical health in the future.

2 Peter Banks suggests that in order to reduce the health risks caused by pollution people should
  A try to live in rural areas and commute to the city for work.
  B make some attempt to leave areas with a lot of pollution.
  C try to live near parks.

3 Why may the elderly find it difficult to live in rural areas?
  A Because there isn't much to do.
  B It may be difficult for them to get to places they need to.
  C There aren't enough facilities.

4 Younger people may find it stressful living in rural areas because
  A they may have to travel to their job.
  B there are very few jobs in rural areas.
  C there is a high rate of unemployment in the countryside.

5 Peter Banks feels that there are
  A more benefits to living in rural areas.
  B more benefits to living in the city.
  C a similar number of benefits to living in the city and in the countryside.

6 According to Peter Banks, the best thing about living in the city is
  A that it is a great place to make new friends.
  B that everything is accessible.
  C people don't tend to use their car as much.

7 The report revealed that people living in rural areas were more positive because
  A they enjoyed being outdoors more.
  B they felt important within their community.
  C they were happy with their standard of living.

Reading and Use of English Part 3

For questions 1–8, read the text below. Use the word given in capitals at the end of some of the lines to form a word that fits in the gap in the same line. There is an example at the beginning (0).

Exercising the Mind

Regular physical activity is certainly good for your body. However, it is also incredibly **(0)** _beneficial_ for the mind. Studies have found that regular exercise can reduce anxiety, stress and **(1)** .... Also, the good news is that regular moderate activity is just as good for your **(2)** .... health as an intensive work out is. For example, a fast-paced walk several times a week, can be just as **(3)** .... for the mind as a regular run would be.

(4) .... , research has also shown that exercise can actually **(5)** .... our mind as well as our body. This is because more exercise can encourage a better blood supply to the brain. **(6)** .... , this means that the level of oxygen and energy supply is also greater, and this results in an individual being able to perform better.

However, **(7)** .... also warn that the positive effects of exercise can easily be lost, once we stop exercising **(8)** ....

BENEFIT

DEPRESS

PSYCHOLOGY

EFFECT

FURTHER
STRONG

CONSEQUENT

RESEARCH

REGULAR

Reading and Use of English Part 2

Read the whole text again when you have finished to make sure that the words you have written make sense.

Exam Info

For questions 1–8, read the text and think of the word which best fits each gap. Use only one word in each gap. There is an example at the beginning (0).

Teenagers need their sleep

The effects of insufficient sleep **(0)** ....on.......... teenagers can be quite dramatic, even more so than in adults, as according **(1)** .... research, young people are biologically driven to require more sleep. A lack **(2)** .... sleep for teenagers can cause low mood, behavioural problems **(3)** .... an inability to concentrate.

A recent report revealed that teenagers not sleeping enough was, **(4)** .... fact, becoming an increasingly significant issue. Researchers found that the average amount of sleep that teenagers get is between 7 and 7.25 hours per **(5)** .... However, studies show that teenagers actually need 9.25 hours of sleep in **(6)** .... to function well, physically and psychologically.

The report also highlighted that the number of teenagers suffering from sleep-related issues **(7)** .... increased dramatically over the last ten years. The reasons **(8)** .... this are varied, and include some of the following: poor habits, poor diet, stress, anxiety and a lack of guidance.

10 On the money

Grammar
Modals expressing ability

1. **Complete these sentences with *can*, *could* or the correct form of *able to*. For some of these sentences there is more than one possibility.**

   1. He ....*could / was able to*.... buy what he wanted, because he had been saving for months.
   2. If you .... (not) get home, I will happily lend you money for the bus fare.
   3. In order to .... afford a new bike, I need to work every weekend.
   4. You .... earn quite a lot of money in this job, if you are willing to work weekends.
   5. Last night, she .... persuade her parents to increase her pocket money.
   6. I .... go shopping and not buy anything, but I wouldn't enjoy it as much.
   7. Her parents have taught her how to budget, so in the future she .... handle her money responsibly.
   8. There is a prize for the team who .... raise the most money for charity.
   9. He doesn't need much in life and .... live on very little money.
   10. She .... (not) buy anything online, as she hasn't had the internet for weeks.

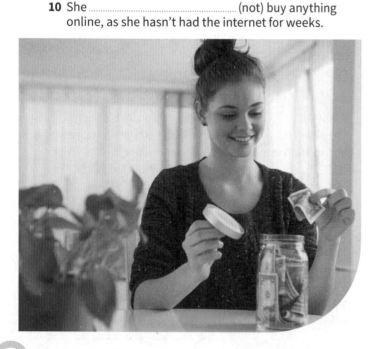

as and like

2. **Are *as* and *like* used correctly in these sentences? Correct any mistakes and put a tick (✓) next to the sentences which are correct.**

   1. As you know, I don't spend too much on myself. ......✓......
   2. My cousin works like a financial advisor. ....
   3. The price of this is the same like it was in the other shop. ....
   4. Your new trainers look like they were very expensive. ....
   5. Shopping online isn't as going to the shops. ....
   6. Selling your possessions isn't as rewarding like donating them to charity. ....
   7. This doesn't look as the sort of thing I want to buy. ....
   8. I paid back my loan as soon as I could. ....

Vocabulary
arrive, get and reach

1. **Circle the correct word in italics.**

   1. Did you manage to *reach* / (*get*) / *arrive* to the bank before it closed?
   2. After months of saving, Paul managed to *arrive* / *get* / *reach* his target goal.
   3. My parents haven't *arrived* / *got* / *reached* a decision yet about buying me a car.
   4. My wages *get* / *reach* / *arrive* in my account every month on the same day.
   5. I am not interested in *getting* / *reaching* / *arriving* rich.
   6. We *get* / *reached* / *arrived* at the house, only to discover it had already been sold!
   7. I couldn't *get* / *reach* / *arrive* her by phone, so I sent her an email instead.
   8. Can you *reach* / *arrive* / *get* the top shelf? I'm too short!

Shopping

2 Read a conversation between Isobel (I) and the shop assistants (SA). Complete the dialogue by choosing one word from the box for each gap.

> customer service receipt exchange guarantee
> purchase label brands discounts stock
> bargain refund sale ~~return~~

I: Excuse me, I bought a dress from this shop last week and I'd like to **(1)** _return_ it, do you know where I can do this?

SA 1: Yes, certainly. If you go to the **(2)** .... department on the third floor, they will be able to help you there.

I: Great, thank you.

SA 2: Hello, how can I help you?

I: Hi, I bought this dress, but I'd like to return it.

SA 2: Ok, that's fine. Do you have the **(3)** ....?

I: Yes, here it is.

SA 2: Thank you. Can I ask what was wrong with the dress?

I: It didn't fit very well, it was too small.

SA 2: Would you like to **(4)** .... it for a bigger size or would you like a full **(5)** ....?

I: Could I have the money please? I am not sure it would suit me anyway.

SA 2: Yes, that's not a problem at all. We **(6)** .... you'll get your money back as long as you return the garment within 28 days of **(7)** .... and it isn't damaged or hasn't been worn.

I: No it hasn't been worn, I couldn't even get it on. I bought it from your online store, so didn't have a chance to try it on.

SA 2: I wouldn't worry, this **(8)** .... always comes up small, in comparison to other **(9)** .... We have a **(10)** .... on today, with some big **(11)** ...., 50% in some lines, so you might see something else you like. The store is trying to get rid of all its winter **(12)** ...., in order to make space for the spring season.

I: Really? Yes, I will have a look, I love a **(13)** ....!

SA2: Could you just print and sign your name here please? Here is your receipt and your money. Hope you find something else you like.

Phrasal verbs

3 Read the text below and complete using the correct form of the phrasal verbs from the box.

> carry out fill in get into open up put in
> run out of set up ~~take out~~

Having your own bank account

In the UK a child can have their own bank account between the ages of eleven and eighteen, although some banks only offer them to children who are sixteen and over. With these current accounts money can be **(1)** _taken out_ or **(2)** .... using a debit card. Fortunately, however, these accounts do not offer an overdraft, so a child is not allowed to borrow money and **(3)** .... debt. If the child is under the age of sixteen, then parents will need to **(4)** .... the account. They can do this by either **(5)** .... a meeting at a bank or by **(6)** .... a form online.

Either way, they will be asked to provide several forms of documentation proving the child's age and identity. Once they have a bank account, they can **(7)** .... the same functions as other bank accounts. Young people can see how much money they have by looking at their statement online or by receiving text messages. This means that they can see if they have **(8)** .... money or if they have enough to still withdraw cash.

You are going to read an article about several teenage entrepreneurs and how they made their money. Choose from the sentences A–G the one which fits each gap (1–6). There is one extra sentence which you do not need to use.

TEENAGE ENTREPRENEURS

You don't need age or experience on your side to set up your own business venture and make money. As these teenagers prove, all you need is determination and a good idea (and perhaps a little help from your parents).

Fraser Doherty, also known as 'JamBoy', set up the company SuperJam when he was just fourteen. He started by selling his grandmother's jam recipe to farmers' markets and delicatessens, before eventually developing his own recipe, which was made solely from fruit. After developing the product and brand further, in 2007 Fraser's SuperJam went on the supermarket giant Waitrose's shelves. **1** More recently, he has also released two books: one which shares his jam-making secrets and the other which tells the story of how he created his business. Both books have become bestsellers.

SuperJam and Fraser Doherty have also won numerous awards. **2** The company also invests in running charitable 'Tea Parties' for the elderly who live alone, in care homes or in sheltered housing.

In 2014, at the age of twelve, Bella Tipping created KidzCationz, a holiday website designed specifically for children. She came up with the idea after a disappointing holiday to America, where she found the food and facilities for kids were just not up to standard. Bella wanted to write about her holiday but was unable to as other travel websites at the time were too adult-focussed. **3** Bella, who comes from Australia, was initially helped by her parents, who invested $80,000 in the project's initial set up. Bella's motto is, 'If you can think it, you can do it.'

Growing up in New York, Noa Mitz decided that she didn't like her nanny, so at the age of twelve she came up with the idea of launching her own babysitting service. She started by finding nannies for family friends and then the business grew from there. It wasn't long before she had established a trusted and sought-after childcare brand. Nannies by Noa serves the residents of New York and the Hamptons and works by pairing clients with a suitable babysitter or nanny. **4** The company is now estimated to be worth $375,000 and Noa is now so busy that she has recently hired a CEO.

Brennan Agranoff is still a high school student, but last year he made over $1 million, selling designer athletic socks. The company is called HoopSwagg and was founded when he was just thirteen years old. **5** After months of research Brennan started the business in his family garage and asked his parents to invest $3,000. Today he runs the business with seventeen staff and his mother. **6**

A The business charges anything between $50 and $100 per match.

B Having identified this gap in the market, this young entrepreneur created the opportunity for other kids to be able to do the same.

C The idea for the venture when born when the teenager noticed that there was a demand for this particular product amongst fellow pupils.

D There are plans to expand the company even further, offering products such as shoelaces and ties.

E It has even gained status in the National Museum of Scotland as it has become an iconic Scottish brand.

F Currently, the product is being sold in over 2,000 stores around the world.

G This brand quickly gained popularity through social media.

Listening Part 1

You will hear people talking in eight different situations. For questions 1–8, choose the best answer (A, B or C).

1 You hear a teenage daughter talking to her dad. Why does the daughter need more money?
   A for concert tickets
   B for something to wear to the concert
   C for some shoes

2 You overhear a mum talking to her son about pocket money. What is the main reason for giving him pocket money?
   A so he does a few jobs around the house
   B to appreciate the importance of money
   C to learn to be sensible with money

3 You overhear a woman talking to the waiter about her bill. What is the woman complaining about?
   A the standard of the service
   B the price of a salad and a drink
   C being charged for the service on the bill

4 You hear a man talking about something he has recently bought online. What does he think about shopping online?
   A It is not as good as going to a shopping centre.
   B It is disappointing.
   C It is easy to use.

5 You hear two teenagers talking about their shopping trip. How does the boy feel afterwards?
   A regretful
   B tired
   C relieved

6 You overhear two friends talking to each other about what kind of job they want in the future. What advice does the girl give about choosing a career?
   A Choose a job that you enjoy.
   B Don't work long hours.
   C Choose a job which gives you enough money to live on.

7 You overhear a boy talking about wanting to buy a new bike. Where is he getting most of the money for his bike from?
   A his part-time job in the summer
   B his parents
   C saving his pocket money

8 You overhear a conversation between a married couple. What is the main reason the man's wife still carries so much cash?
   A It is something she has always done.
   B She is worried that some places don't take cards.
   C She is worried she will have to pay more for using her card.

Reading and Use of English Part 3

For questions 1–8, read the text below. Use the word given in capitals at the end of some of the lines to form a word that fits in the gap in the same line. There is an example at the beginning (0).

Buying things will not make you happy

The advertising industry and (0) _economists_ may have us believe that we need to (1) .... consume in order to feel happy and good about ourselves. However, of course, this is not the case, and owning possessions does not bring you (2) ....

ECONOMY
CONSTANT

HAPPY

When first bought, the item might be at the (3) .... of fashion, but it will soon be replaced by the latest model. Sometimes, it is also believed that friends and family will find our new purchases (4) .... However, this is (5) .... the case. Even people who can afford whatever they want are not always happy and this is proof that (6) .... cannot be found through possessions. Mass buying also leads to (7) .... problems and by buying too much our society is currently creating too much waste material such as packaging.

HIGH

IMPRESS
RARE

SATISFY

ENVIRONMENT

In order to feel happier and to help the environment, people need to place less (8) .... on buying things and focus more on what really matters.

IMPORTANT

11 Medical matters

Grammar

Relative pronouns and relative clauses

1a Complete the sentences with the correct relative pronoun from the box.

> which   who   whose   where

1 People ....*who*........ want to have a healthy lifestyle should eat well and exercise regularly.
2 This is the hospital .... I was born.
3 A thermometer is the object .... you use to check your temperature.
4 That is the surgeon .... is going to perform the operation.
5 People .... blood pressure is too high need to be careful about what they eat.
6 His dad, ... is a doctor, is well-respected in the medical profession.
7 This is the medicine .... I must take regularly.
8 There are many clubs .... young people can join in order to stay active.
9 People .... diet is poor are at a greater risk of health problems.
10 This is the department .... patients come if they have a medical emergency.

1b Which sentence contains a non-defining relative clause?

1c In which sentences can the relative pronoun can be replaced by *that*?

1d In which sentences can the relative pronouns can be omitted?

1e Read the following pair of sentences. Which person has more than one cousin? Why?

(i) My cousin, who is a nurse, works in the local hospital. (non-defining relative clause)
(ii) My cousin who is a nurse works in the local hospital. (defining relative clause)

2 Match the two halves of the sentences.

1 My brother has a prescription from the doctor,
2 I was frightened of having injections,
3 If your temperature gets too high,
4 When I have a headache,
5 When I fell over at school,
6 He had a swollen ankle,

A I was given a plaster by the nurse.
B you should go to the doctor.
C I always take some aspirin.
D so he had to stop and rest.
E but I am used to them now.
F so he has to go to the chemist's to pick it up.

1	2	3 ....
4	5	6 ....

Vocabulary

arrive, get and *reach*

1 What are the noun forms of these adjectives?

complicated	*complication.*	loyal	....
polite	....	energetic	....
encouraging	....	perfect	....
concerned	....	significant	....
courageous	....	memorable	....
accurate	....	kind	....
comfortable	....	possible	....

2 Now write the negative of the adjective forms in the correct column.

dis	im	in	un
	impossible		

Writing Part 1

Developing an argument

1 Read part of the first draft of a student's answer to this essay.

In your English class, you have been talking about the growing problem of childhood obesity, partly due to young people eating too much junk food. Now, your English teacher has asked you to write an essay.

Write an essay using all the notes and give reasons for your point of view.

Essay question
Some doctors feel that fast food restaurants should be banned from opening near schools.

Why is this the case? Do you agree?

Notes
Write about:
1 fast food / obesity
2 convenience
3 your own idea

In Writing Part 1 it is important to expand on the points you make, by giving supporting statements or examples.

Exam Info

2 Add the sentences or clauses (A–F) to the correct part of the essay (1–3). There are three extra sentences which do not match.

A it is very easy for them to buy junk food from the local fast food shop

B therefore, the problem of obesity would get worse

C cooking lessons would also develop this awareness

D which makes it difficult for them to make healthy decisions

E who are still in the process of growing and developing

F they go home and have their dinner

In order to tackle the growing problem of childhood obesity, doctors are now recommending that all fast food restaurants be banned from opening near schools. This is because eating junk food regularly is very unhealthy; especially for young people, (1) .... A diet of fish, chips, burgers and fried chicken may sound very appealing, but it can cause obesity or other health-related issues.

It is not surprising, therefore, that the medical profession is requesting that fast food restaurants should not be located near schools. Currently, buying junk food is far too convenient for many pupils and when they finish school, often hungry, (2) ....

I strongly agree with this recommendation given by doctors, as it is very tempting for pupils to buy junk food after school. What's more, there is a need for education. Nutrition lessons in school would help young people become more informed about the food they choose. Similarly, (3) ....

Reading and Use of English Part 3

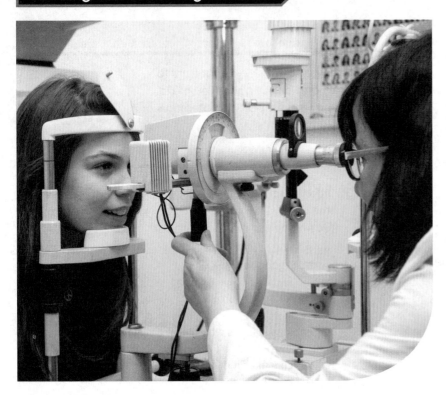
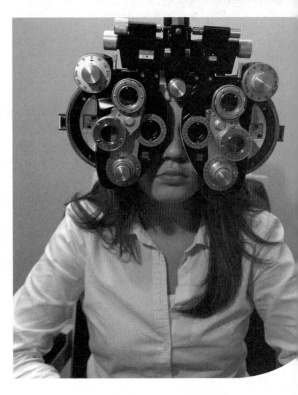

For questions 1–8, read the text below. Use the words given in capitals at the end of some of the lines to form a word that fits in the space in the same line. There is an example at the beginning (0).

Looking after your eyes

Having your eyes tested doesn't just assess your **(0)** ....*ability*........ to see – it is also very useful at checking your overall health. Going for an eye test can detect many general health problems even before any symptoms occur.

ABLE

(1) ...., opticians recommend that most people have an eye test at least every two years. An average eye

GENERAL

(2) .... takes around twenty minutes and consists of several tests which the optician uses to assess your vision and health. The test usually starts with a **(3)** .... about your lifestyle and any changes you may have noticed with your vision.

EXAM

DISCUSS

(4) .... on your age, the optician will then perform a series of **(5)** .... The task which is most familiar to people is when you are asked to read letters from a chart to assess your range of **(6)** ....

DEPEND

ASSESS

SEE

(7) .... the tests are finished, the optician will give you your results and you may be given a **(8)** .... for a pair of glasses or some different lenses.

ONE

PRESCRIBE

Reading and Use of English Part 4

For questions 1–6, complete the second sentence so that it has a similar meaning to the first sentence, using the word given. Do not change the word given. You must use between two and five words, including the word given. Here is an example (0).

Example:

0 I would go out tonight but I am still recovering from the flu.

OVER

I can't go out tonight as I am still
...............*getting over*............... the flu.

1 Having more activity in life makes people healthier.

IF

People live more ....
more active.

2 'I think you should rest,' said the doctor.

ADVISED

The doctor ....some
rest.

3 Her plan is to eat more healthily in the future.

LIKE

She would ....food in
the future.

4 My last cold was much worse than this one.

BAD

This cold is ....the last
one I had.

5 Several specialists have examined my injury.

SEEN

My injury ....by
several specialists.

6 Injections aren't usually painful, but I don't like having them.

THOUGH

I don't like having injections
..............................usually hurt.

Listening Part 4

You will hear a high-school student interviewing the school nurse as part of her research project. For questions 1–7, choose the best answer (A, B or C).

1 The school nurse needs to carry out duties
  A just in the senior school.
  B in many schools.
  C in three schools.

2 The role of school nurse involves
  A regularly checking students' teeth.
  B giving students advice on being healthy.
  C making sure every student has seen the dentist.

3 In her assessments, the school nurse needs to check
  A eyesight.
  B height.
  C level of fitness.

4 If students have any health worries, they can
  A see her before or after school.
  B see her during office hours.
  C contact her to arrange a time to meet .

5 What is a normal day like for the school nurse?
  A She spends every day encouraging young people to be healthy.
  B Her days vary a lot.
  C She meets lots of different people.

6 Why does she think it is harder for younger people to be healthy?
  A They have fewer opportunities to do sport.
  B Many young people spend a lot of time on electronic devices.
  C They have bad diets.

7 How do most parents react when they are told their child needs to change their eating habits?
  A They are annoyed.
  B They feel embarrassed.
  C They are thankful that they have been told.

12 Animal kingdom

Grammar

Third conditional

1   Read about how Tom's dog became part of their family. Complete the sentences with the correct form of the verbs in brackets.

1   If I ......*had not forgotten*...... (not forgot) my lunch box, I ......*wouldn't have gone*...... (not go) back home.

2   If I .... (not see) a stray dog at the side of the road, my mum .... (not stop) the car.

3   If the dog .... (not be) so friendly, we .... (not take) him home.

4   If we .... (not help) him, he .... (be) run over.

5   If he .... (be) collected by his owner, we .... (not keep) him.

6   If he .... (not become) part of our family, I .... (be) very sad.

wish, if only and hope

2   Complete each sentence with *wish* or *hope*.

1   I ......*hope*...... you understand the responsibility involved in looking after a pet.

2   I .... you could have experienced swimming with dolphins.

3   I .... you get to see elephants on your trip.

4   One day I .... to go on safari in Africa.

5   I .... everyone would stop trying to persuade me to go horse riding.

6   I .... the animals are well looked after in this zoo.

7   I .... people would give more thought to animal conservation.

8   I .... she doesn't bring her cat, I just don't like them.

9   I .... I am not interrupting you, but I think that bird is trying to eat your lunch.

10 I .... we lived in an apartment where pets are allowed.

3   If a pair of sentences has the same meaning, put a tick (✓) next to them. If they have different meanings, rewrite the second sentence so it means the same as the first.

1   a   It's a shame I wasn't interested in animals as a child, I could have been a vet.

    b   If only I ~~hadn't~~ been interested in animals when I was young, I could have become a vet.   ......✗ *had*......

2   a   We wanted to stay at the zoo longer, but we were just too tired.

    b   If we had been so tired, we would have stayed at the zoo longer.   ....

3   a   I regret not having a pet when I was young.

    b   I wish I had had a pet when I was a child.   ....

4   a   I really want a pet rabbit, I would really look after it.

    b   If only I could have a pet rabbit, I would really take care of it.   ....

Vocabulary

avoid, prevent and protect; check, control and supervise

1 Circle the correct word in each sentence.

1 When you are in the sea you should *prevent* / *avoid* being stung by jellyfish.
2 When young children are feeding animals they should be *checked* / *supervised* at all times.
3 Sometimes if my dog sees a cat, he is difficult to *control* / *supervise*.
4 It is our responsibility to *prevent* / *avoid* certain species from becoming extinct.
5 The zoo vet needs to *check* / *control* the health of the animals regularly.
6 We must *protect* / *prevent* animals from increasing levels of pollution.

Writing Part 2

An email

1 Look at the beginnings of five sentences below. Choose endings from A–E, which all give advice about becoming involved with an animal charity.

1 The best idea
2 So I suggest you look
3 Make sure that you
4 My advice to you is
5 If I were you, I

A would see which option interests you the most.
B would be for you to look at our website.
C to get involved in our activities for kids.
D at all the information and discuss it with your parents.
E always get permission from an adult beforehand.

1 .... 2 .... 3 ....
4 .... 5 ....

2 Now read the email. Complete each gap with one of the sentences from Exercise 1.

To: Katie

From: Mathew Thompson

Dear Katie,

Thank you for contacting us and expressing your wish to help with our animal charity.

In your email you mentioned that you would like to volunteer to help with animals in need.

As you are under sixteen, I am afraid there are limited opportunities to do this. Fortunately, however, we do have a number of other ways you can become part of our organisation.
(i) .... This way you can learn more about animals and about what we do.

(ii) .... This gives details of all the activities available to someone your age.

On the site there is a whole selection of activities you can become involved with. You could subscribe to our animal magazine, enter our animal photography competition or just find out more about animals. **(iii)** .... Furthermore, the website gives you some tips on how to fundraise for our charity. For example, you could organise an animal quiz and charge people to enter, or you could make biscuits or cakes to sell to family and friends. **(iv)** .... Any money that you raise will help to rescue and rehome the many animals in need. **(v)** .... Good luck and do not hesitate to contact us if you have any further questions.

Best wishes,

Mathew Thompson

You are going to read an article from a magazine about getting a pet as a present. For questions 1–6, choose the answer (A, B, C or D) which you think fits best according to the text.

A DOG iS FOR LiFE!

Every year the number of dogs bought increases during the festive period, as many people see them as an ideal present for their loved one. It is true, that for the right person and environment they can make a fantastic gift, one that can be loved and looked after every day. Unfortunately, however, a lot of them can also soon become an unwanted gift, and animal charities have recently reported a significant increase in the number of dogs abandoned just after the New Year. According to some campaigners, this issue is getting worse and not better, mainly as a result of social media. Social media sites are used by celebrities and others to display their dogs online without mentioning any of the responsibilities that are involved in looking after these pets. This has led to other people wanting to purchase dogs and show them off in their online posts and photographs. People doing this have also been assisted by it being easier to buy dogs over the internet. Understandably, therefore, animal charities are once again reminding people to think before they buy a dog as a gift. In this article we will look at some of the things which should be considered before purchasing a dog as a present.

Before choosing to invest in a dog, you must first consider whether you have enough time, money and energy for one. Puppies, in particular, can be very demanding at first and, more significantly, you will need a great deal of energy and patience to teach them. Puppies are brand new to the world and will need to be taught how to behave around people and objects. Don't be surprised if they try to tear up your carpets initially, or chew on your favourite pair of shoes.

Dogs can also be very costly in their first year, as they will need good quality to food to help them grow. Furthermore, puppies will also require some medical attention, as they will need their initial course of vaccinations and an annual check-up at the very least. If they become sick, then you will need money for the vet fees. Many animal charities now recommend that people invest in pet insurance in order to cover these costs.

Time is another major factor to consider when buying a dog. Dogs are social animals and don't like to be left alone, so make sure that you will not have to leave them for long periods of time. Also, they need plenty of exercise, so you will need to factor this into your daily routine and ensure that your dog has regular walks. Finally, when you go on holiday, your dog will need to be cared for, so you must make arrangements for them to be looked after: either by a friend or at a kennel (a holiday home for dogs).

It is also recommended that before buying a dog, you think carefully about what breed of dog would be best for you. Dogs come in a lot of different shapes and sizes, and so it is important to consider which type would be most suited to your living space. It wouldn't be appropriate to have a big dog, for example, if you lived in a small flat with no garden. Dogs have different levels of energy and personalities, and this should also be considered.

For instance, Springer Spaniels need a great deal of exercise, so they would be best avoided if you don't have the time to cater for this. It may also be worth investigating any health problems that are common in the particular breed which interests you.

Dogs can make wonderful gifts, but just make sure you are aware of the amount of work involved and that you do plenty of research beforehand. Deciding to buy one shouldn't be a decision which is taken lightly.

1 What happens to many dogs in the New Year?
   A They are given to animal charities.
   B They are looked after well.
   C They are left without a home.
   D They are given to new owners.

2 The article states that more people are buying dogs as gifts than ever before. What is the principle reason for this?
   A Because they are easy to buy online.
   B Because dogs have become popular with many famous people.
   C Because of social networking sites.
   D Because people are unaware of the responsibilities involved.

3 Owning a puppy is more challenging than having an older dog because
   A they are likely to be ill in their first year.
   B they will need to be trained.
   C they will need to be supervised at all times.
   D they are more expensive to maintain.

4 Dogs should not be left alone for long periods of time because
   A they need to be fed regularly.
   B by nature they like company.
   C they need frequent exercise.
   D they may destroy the furniture.

5 Apart from the size, what else do you need to consider when choosing a breed?
   A where they come from
   B their cost
   C their personality
   D the size of your garden

6 According to the article, a dog should only be bought if
   A you fully understand what having one means.
   B you are prepared to work very hard.
   C you choose the right breed.
   D you discuss the decision carefully with others .

Listening Part 2

13 You will hear a man called Jacob giving a talk on how he became a jockey. For questions 1–10, complete the sentences with a word or short phrase.

Becoming a jockey

At first, Jacob's mother and father were
(1) .... that horseracing wasn't safe.

His first training course was (2) .... , so he spent a lot of time with fellow jockeys.

When he was doing his course he had to look after
(3) .... horses.

Before he started his course he thought that all the trainees would be (4) .... riders.

The main (5) .... for the course is that you are not too heavy or tall.

After graduating from his course, Jacob was
(6) .... with an appropriate employer.

After he completed his course he received a licence to compete as a (7) .... jockey.

You need to be physically fit and (8) .... in the methods you use in different situations.

Horses can have different personalities, so Jacob needs to know how to (9) .... every horse he rides.

If Jacob's salary was to increase in the future he would be
(10) ....

13 House space

Grammar

Causative *have* and *get*

Before

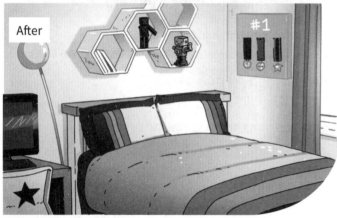

After

1a A teenage boy wants to have his bedroom decorated. Look at the 'Before' picture. What does he need to do to change it? Complete the sentences with the correct form of the verbs from the box.

> removed ~~put up~~ replaced attached painted

1 He needs to ......*have*...... shelves ......*put up*...... above his bed.
2 He is going to .... the old wallpaper ....
3 He wants to .... the walls .... white.
4 He wants to .... a board for his medals .... to the wall.
5 He needs to .... the old curtains .... with new ones.

1b Now, look at the 'After' picture. Write sentences to describe what the boy has done to decorate his room.

6 *He has had shelves put up above his bed.*
7 ....
8 ....
9 ....
10 ....

Expressing obligation and permission

2 Circle the correct words in each sentence.

1 Take your shoes off at the door you *needn't /* *are not supposed to* wear them in the house.
2 Before leaving the house you *must / should* make sure the iron has been turned off. You forgot to do it yesterday.
3 You *mustn't / don't have to* dust that shelf, as the cleaner is coming tomorrow.
4 We *shouldn't / were supposed to* have moved in two months ago, but things got delayed.
5 I am only *allowed / required* to use the cooker when my parents are around, otherwise it isn't safe.
6 Mum says I *needn't / can't* go out until my room is tidy.
7 I *couldn't / shouldn't* visit my friend's house because it was too far to walk.
8 You *needn't / mustn't* go to the shops, I am sure the neighbours have some sugar we could borrow.
9 Before buying a new computer, you *must / could* do your research, otherwise you might get a bad deal.
10 My new teacher is very demanding, and I *can / have to* do a lot of homework.

at, *in* and *on* to express location

3 Complete the sentences with the correct preposition: *in, on, at.*

1 When you arrive, please park ....*on*........ the other side of the street.
2 I haven't got enough space on the shelves, I'll need to put my books .... a box.
3 I think we should put the picture .... this wall.
4 When I come home from school, my dog is always waiting for me .... the door.
5 There is some more jam .... the fridge.
6 Your clothes for tomorrow are .... the end of your bed.
7 When you have finished dinner please put your plates .... the dishwasher.

Vocabulary

Collocations

1 Circle the correct word in each sentence.

1 I love my bedroom because it is really *vast* / ⟨*spacious*⟩
2 My *ideal* / *best* home would overlook the sea.
3 We are going away for the summer, so the house will be left *abandoned* / *vacant*.
4 Our apartment is *situated* / *placed* right in the city centre.
5 I hate sharing a bedroom; mum should *transform* / *convert* the loft into another bedroom.
6 I thought the cottage we stayed in was really *cosy* / *friendly*.
7 The *value* / *worth* of our house has really increased.
8 This part of town has become a very *desirable* / *recommended* place to live.
9 This architecture of this old house is truly *magnificent* / *brilliant*.
10 The furniture in the house was very *ancient* / *old-fashioned* and she couldn't wait to change it.

Listening Part 4

 You will hear a psychologist talking on the radio about the best ways to help a teenager through the process of moving house. For questions 1–7, choose the best answer (A, B or C).

1 Moving house can be particularly hard for teenagers because
  A they have to transfer to a new school.
  B it is hard for them to start new friendships.
  C of the stage of life they are in.

2 What is Penny's advice for parents who have not yet chosen a house?
  A to choose a property which their teenager approves of
  B to ask their teenager for their ideas on the new property and area
  C to choose a neighbourhood which their teenager likes

3 What is the main piece of advice which she gives to families moving to a new area?
  A Parents should research new clubs for their teenager to join.
  B Parents should speak to teenagers about their emotions.
  C Teenagers should choose their new school.

4 Why should teenagers join new clubs in the area?
  A so that parents have more time to themselves
  B so they can enjoy doing an activity they are good at
  C so they can meet classmates before starting school

5 How can parents best help teenagers feel better about moving away from their friends?
  A arrange a goodbye party
  B arrange a trip to see old friends in the near future
  C buy them a scrap book, to keep contact details in

6 What does Penny suggest a teenager should do a few weeks before moving?
  A make a list of things they need to do
  B sell the things they don't want
  C complete the list of tasks given to them

7 On moving day itself, why should teenagers be given a specific job to do?
  A so they feel a sense of achievement
  B because their contribution will be useful
  C to keep them as busy as possible

Writing Part 2
Adding detail

1 Read some sentences from an article a teenager wrote about her favourite room in the house: her bedroom. Then match them to the type of detail they provide (A–F).

1   I am relaxed and happy when I am in there because I can arrange it how I want.

2   I have posters on the walls of all the things I like, and pictures of friends pinned to a board.

3   I moved into the room last year, just after my parents had finished decorating it. It used to be an office.

4   I like the fact that I have the freedom to do what I want in my room. I can practise on my guitar or do some reading.

5   My room isn't quite as big as my sister's, but I don't mind.

6   As a teenager, I think it is really important to have some personal space.

Type of detail

A   providing a description

B   making a comparison

C   giving an opinion

D   giving an example

E   providing facts

F   describing feelings

1 .... 2 .... 3 ....

4 .... 5 .... 6 ....

2 Now look at this examination task.

My favourite room

Tell us about your favourite room and why it's special for you.

The best article will be published in next month's magazine. Write 140–190 words.

3 Plan your answer for this task. What type of detail would you include?

My favourite room:

Fact:

Description:

Feeling:

Opinion:

Comparison:

Example:

4 Use your notes to complete the exam task.

For questions 1–8, read the text below and decide which answer (A, B, C or D)
best fits each gap. There is an example at the beginning (0).

0 A mainly   **(B)** overall   **C** largely   **D** then

Having a Roommate

Since I can remember I have always shared a bedroom with my
older brother. Sharing a room with him has had both advantages
and disadvantages, but **(0)** .... , I would say I actually
quite like it. Our room is quite large, so we each have our own
double bed and a bit of **(1)** .... to keep our things.
Fortunately, we also get on fairly well, so we **(2)** .... argue,
although we do occasionally have small **(3)** .... about
whose turn it is to tidy up. We are quite good at sharing our
(4) .... , like our computer or our toy cars when we were
younger, as we have always had to do this.

Nevertheless, we each have our own wall, so we can
(5) .... it the way we want to. For example, my brother
has all his sports medals hung up on his wall, **(6)** I
have posters of my sporting **(7)** .... on mine. If I was to
move into my own room now, I would probably feel a bit lonely, at
least at first, as I am so used to my brother's **(8)** ....

1	**A**	place	**B**	area	**C**	space	**D** territory
2	**A**	usually	**B**	rarely	**C**	scarcely	**D** extraordinarily
3	**A**	argue	**B**	conversations	**C**	discussions	**D** disagreements
4	**A**	possessions	**B**	objects	**C**	items	**D** gadgets
5	**A**	ornament	**B**	construct	**C**	decorate	**D** furnish
6	**A**	though	**B**	instead	**C**	nevertheless	**D** whereas
7	**A**	team	**B**	people	**C**	heroes	**D** likes
8	**A**	way	**B**	company	**C**	habit	**D** existence

1 Complete the newspaper article below by putting the verbs in brackets into the correct form of the passive.

The school prom is traditionally a formal dance or party which **(1)** _is celebrated_ by high school students when they leave school. It has been part of American culture since the nineteenth century but has only fairly recently become popular in the UK. Over the last two decades the prom tradition has grown rapidly in popularity, and it **(2)** .... (estimate) that currently it **(3)** .... (celebrate) by approximately 85% of all UK schools. Usually the school prom **(4)** .... (associate) with seventeen- or eighteen-year-olds, who are just about to leave school; in the UK however, the prom parties **(5)** .... (throw) by students at different stages in their school life. For example, students who are finishing Year 11 at the age of sixteen can also experience this type of celebration. In some cases, the tradition **(6)** .... (even take up) by some primary schools, as pupils celebrate their move from junior to senior school.

These school proms can **(7)** .... (hold) in the school sports hall or in a five-star hotel. What **(8)** .... (wear) to the prom has become of great importance and parents can **(9)** .... (require) to spend a fortune on a new dress or suit. Transport is also a key part of the event and commonly limousines **(10)** .... (hire) to escort pupils to the party. Last year, it **(11)** .... (report) that one teenage girl decided to make an entrance to her prom by arriving on a horse. It would seem that every year, proms are becoming more popular, more extravagant and indeed more expensive for parents. In fact, it **(12)** .... (estimate) that the cost of prom night has risen by 72% in the last five years.

2 Rewrite the newspaper headlines as sentences, using the verb in brackets. You will need to add some extra words.

1

> The royal wedding will take place in May

It has been announced that the royal wedding will take place in May. (announce)

2

> SCIENTISTS DISCOVER A NEW PLANET

It ....
.... (confirm)

3

> Over 20,000 people attended the outdoor festival this year

Over 20,000 ....
.... (report)

4

> NORWAY HAS THE BEST EDUCATION SYSTEM IN THE WORLD

Norway ....
.... (consider)

5

> Summer will be the warmest on record

It ....
.... (believe)

6

> 'Go out and vote!'
> says the Prime Minister.

The public ....
.... (advise)

Writing Part 1
An essay

1 Read the exam task below and the student answer. Write *this*, *them*, *these*, *those* or *it* in each gap. In some gaps, more than one answer is possible.

> Every year your school holds a three-day arts festival at the end of the summer term to celebrate music, art and drama. Students of all year groups work together on different projects and then the best performances and pieces of work are presented to parents on the final day.
>
> In your English class you have been discussing the benefits of the festival. Now, your English teacher has asked you to write an essay for homework. Write an essay using all the notes and give reasons for your point of view.
>
> **Essay question**
>
> *There are many benefits to having an arts festival each year.*
>
> *Do you agree?*
>
> **Notes**
>
> Write about:
>
> 1 the advantages of the festival
> 2 the possible disadvantages
> 3 .... (your own idea)
>
> Write your essay in 140–190 words.

The arts festival is an important part of the school calendar. **(1)** ....It........ is a a three-day event which celebrates music, art and drama within the school. Students work on projects together over the three days and then they present **(2)** .... to parents on the final day.

There are many benefits to holding this festival at the school. Firstly, **(3)** .... event can encourage teamwork throughout the school, and students of all ages can work together to produce something creative. Secondly, pupils are also given the opportunity to express their talent, in one or more of **(4)** .... areas. Furthermore, **(5)** .... students who don't usually participate in such activities, may discover they have a newfound interest in one of **(6)** .... subjects.

For some students, however, the festival may not be such a positive experience. For example, pupils who don't have any interest in these areas will have to spend three days doing activities they do not enjoy.

Overall, I think that most students benefit from the festival. If they are allowed to choose the area which interests **(7)** .... the most, then **(8)** .... becomes a worthwhile experience.

2 What is the student's own idea in their essay?

3 Choose a word or phrase from the list below to complete the student's essay plan.

- disadvantages of the arts festival
- a recommendation for other projects
- conclusion
- a description of the arts festival
- advantages of the arts festival
- introduction

> **Essay Plan**
> Paragraph 1 ...
> Paragraph 2 ...
> Paragraph 3 ...
> Paragraph 4 ...

Which points are not covered and why?

4 Now write your answer to the question below. Use your own plan or a similar plan to the one in Exercise 3.

> In your English class you have been discussing the end-of-year party for the Year 11 students – the school prom. Now, your English teacher has asked you to write an essay for homework. Write an essay using all the notes and give reasons for your point of view.
>
> **Essay question**
>
> *The school prom should be banned, as it has become too expensive for parents. Instead, pupils should have informal parties, where they are not required to spend money on expensive clothes.*
>
> *Do you agree?*
>
> **Notes**
>
> Write about:
>
> 1 the advantages of having a school prom
> 2 the disadvantages of the school prom
> 3 .... (your own idea)
>
> Write your essay in 140–190 words.

Vocabulary
Word formation – suffixes

Add suffixes to these words to make nouns that describe people. Then underline the word which is the odd one out in each case.

1 bank .... deal ....
   entertain .... consult ....

2 inspect .... profession ....
   solicit .... supervise ....

3 sales .... police ....
   farm .... fire ....

4 history .... account ....
   assist .... attend ....

5 journal .... special ....
   novel .... detect ....

6 music .... politics ....
   research .... electric ....

Listening Part 3

(15) You will hear five short extracts in which people are talking about a celebration they have been to. For questions 1–5, choose from the list (A–H) what each person has celebrated. Use the letters only once. There are three extra letters which you do not need to use.

A a wedding
B passing an exam   Speaker 1 [ ] 1
C getting a new job   Speaker 2 [ ] 2
D winning a race   Speaker 3 [ ] 3
E a retirement party   Speaker 4 [ ] 4
F a birthday party   Speaker 5 [ ] 5
G the end of a school year
H the New Year

Reading and Use of English Part 7

You are going to read some texts about different birthday celebrations. For questions 1–10, choose from the texts (A–E). The texts may be chosen more than once.

Which text mentions

that a sense of national pride is expressed on birthdays? **1**

that everybody attending the event receives a present? **2**

a party game which involves predictions? **3**

that birthday celebrations are mainly shared with relatives? **4**

that the birthday cake is often replaced with something else? **5**

that it is only recently that all birthdays have become more significant? **6**

a custom which started with one incident and then was quickly adopted by other people? **7**

an action which is supposed to affect someone's height? **8**

the birthday boy or girl needs to choose a partner? **9**

a custom which is less popular amongst young people? **10**

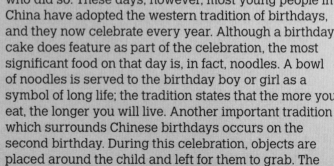

BIRTHDAY CELEBRATIONS Around the World

A China

In the past, people in China did not attach a huge amount of importance to celebrating birthdays, and it was only the very young and elderly who did so. These days, however, most young people in China have adopted the western tradition of birthdays, and they now celebrate every year. Although a birthday cake does feature as part of the celebration, the most significant food on that day is, in fact, noodles. A bowl of noodles is served to the birthday boy or girl as a symbol of long life; the tradition states that the more you eat, the longer you will live. Another important tradition which surrounds Chinese birthdays occurs on the second birthday. During this celebration, objects are placed around the child and left for them to grab. The items chosen are then supposed to give some indication as to the child's future. For example, if a child chooses a doll, then they will have many children, or if they pick up money, then they will be wealthy in the future.

B Russia

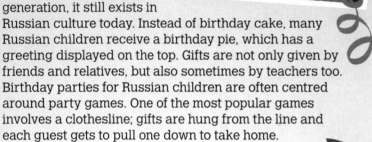

Russia also has many unique birthday traditions. For example, when it is your birthday it is common to have some older friends or relatives to pull your ears. They usually pull your ears upwards to ensure that you will grow taller. Although this tradition is more common with the older generation, it still exists in Russian culture today. Instead of birthday cake, many Russian children receive a birthday pie, which has a greeting displayed on the top. Gifts are not only given by friends and relatives, but also sometimes by teachers too. Birthday parties for Russian children are often centred around party games. One of the most popular games involves a clothesline; gifts are hung from the line and each guest gets to pull one down to take home.

C Norway

In Norway, when it is someone's birthday the country's flag is displayed outside their house. Also, when important people have birthdays they decorate the street with flags. Like many other countries, the Norwegians have a special birthday song. However, it is also accompanied by a special birthday dance. For birthday celebrations at school, Norwegian children are usually asked to dance with a friend in front of the class, whilst the other students sing the birthday song. A common game at birthday parties is 'fishing for ice cream'; guests are asked to fish for frozen gifts, which are attached to pieces of string.

D Jamaica

In Jamaica birthday celebrations can be very messy. This is because in Jamaica there is a tradition which involves throwing flour at the person whose birthday it is, regardless of their age. As the weather in Jamaica is often very hot and humid, this can also make the flour very sticky. The tradition first emerged as a harmless joke played by a school boy. However, the custom quickly became popular throughout Jamaica and loved ones can spend days planning how best to surprise the birthday boy or girl.

E Mexico

Mexican birthday celebrations can be very lively events and centre very much around the family. One of the most popular traditions is 'la mordida.' This is when the person celebrating has their hands tied behind their back, and then they are encouraged to take the first bite of their cake. 'Mordida' is the Spanish word for bribe, but this local term is used in birthday celebrations to mean 'taking a bite'. As the birthday boy or girl begins to eat their cake, the people around them shout 'Mordida! Mordida! Mordida!' Mexican birthday cakes can be quite impressive and they are usually very colourful and very creamy.

Acknowledgements

The authors and publishers acknowledge the following sources of copyright material and are grateful for the permissions granted. While every effort has been made, it has not always been possible to identify the sources of all the material used, or to trace all copyright holders. If any omissions are brought to our notice, we will be happy to include the appropriate acknowledgements on reprinting and in the next update to the digital edition, as applicable.

Key: U = Unit

Photography

All the photographs are sourced from Getty Images.

U1: JasonDoiy/iStock/Getty Images Plus; sedmak/iStock Editorial/Getty Images Plus; Mike Hewitt/Getty Images News; Caiaimage/Paul Bradbury; moodboard/Getty Images Plus; praetorianphoto/E+; **U2**: Jutta Klee/The Image Bank; Jenny Acheson/Photodisc; dolgachov/iStock/Getty Images Plus; John & Lisa Merrill/Photodisc; Yoshikazu Tsuno/AFP; nelik/iStock/Getty Images Plus; Paul Biris/Moment; gloriasalgado/RooM; Adriana Varela Photography/Moment; **U3**: Derek Croucher/Photographer's Choice; Sir Francis Canker Photography/Moment; Katja Kreder/AWL Images; Jan Kopec/The Image Bank; South_agency/E+; **U4**: monkeybusinessimages/iStock/Getty Images Plus; David M. Benett/Getty Images Entertainment; Steve Debenport/iStock/Getty Images Plus; Jupiterimages/Stockbyte; **U5**: Igor Emmerich/Image Source; MIXA; **U6**: Michelangelo Gratton/DigitalVision; ymgerman/iStock Editorial/Getty Images Plus; ptaxa/iStock/Getty Images Plus; 123ducu/iStock/Getty Images Plus; **U7**: Tom Bol; Jodie Griggs/Taxi; MediaProduction/iStock/Getty Images Plus; Graiki/Moment; Marco Bieri/EyeEm; **U8**: monkeybusinessimages/iStock/Getty Images Plus; BrettCharlton/iStock Unreleased; Olaf Herschbach/EyeEm Premium; halbergman/E+; **U9**: Hill Street Studios/Blend Images; Tom Merton/OJO Images; Inti St Clair/Blend Images; Klubovy/iStock/Getty Images Plus; Tetra Images; **U10**: JGI/Jamie Grill/Blend Images; Image Source; Marcelo Aguilar Lopez/EyeEm; **U11**: Martin Hospach; Maica/E+; dlewis33/E+; Jamie Grill/The Image Bank; **U12**: Fnsy/iStock/Getty Images Plus; SolStock/E+; Francisca Höftmann/EyeEm; Bob Thomas/Stone; **U13**: Blanchi Costela/Moment; Karen Moskowitz/The Image Bank; Juan Silva/The Image Bank; **U14**: Hill Street Studios/Blend Images; LWA/Stone; Dreet Production/Alloy; stockstudioX/iStock/Getty Images Plus; theo_stock/iStock/Getty Images Plus; AleksandarGeorgiev/E+.

Front cover photography by ultraforma/E+/Getty Images.

Illustration

Illustration by Carl Pearce

Audio

Audio production by Leon Chambers.

The publishers are also grateful to the following contributors:
Alison Ramsey: Editor
Denise Cowle: Proofreader